"WHAT A DELIGHT. A LOT OF WISDOM AND USEFUL INFORMATION IN A FUN AND READABLE FORM. DAVIS KNOWS WHAT HE IS TALKING ABOUT. IF YOU'RE WILLING TO HAVE YOUR LIFE WORK BETTER, THIS BOOK IS A VALUABLE TOOL KIT."

—JAMES FADIMAN, PH.D.
AUTHOR, UNLIMIT YOUR LIFE: SETTING AND GETTING GOALS.

"THIS BOOK IS AN INVALUABLE RESOURCE FOR ANYONE WHO DESIRES TO MAINTAIN AN EFFECTIVE SELF-IDENTITY, WHERE THERE IS SIMULTANEOUSLY ROOM TO GROW AND LET GO OF OLD WAYS OF BEING, KEVIN DAVIS, A GIFTED EXECUTIVE COACH AND THERAPIST, PROVIDES TOOLS, PRACTICES, EXAMPLES AND GOOD HUMOR TO OUR OWN PERSONAL AND PROFESSIONAL DEVELOPMENT PROCESSES. INSPIRING, REALISTIC, AND AN EFFECTIVE RESOURCE IN MAINTAINING SELF-RESPECT AND SELF-VALUE, NO MATTER WHAT CIRCUMSTANCES WE FACE."

—ANGELES ARRIEN, PH.D.
CULTURAL ANTHROPOLOGIST
AUTHOR OF THE SECOND HALF OF LIFE

"THIS BOOK IS LIKE FINE WINE. THE MORE ONE PARTAKES AND SAVORS THE MESSAGE, THE GREATER THE APPRECIATION AND EFFECT. KEVIN DAVIS CONTENDS THAT IT IS NOT A "HOW TO" BOOK NOR IS IT AN INSPIRATIONAL BOOK. HOWEVER, THE NINE FUNDAMENTALS OF HUMAN BEHAVIOR CAN EASILY OFFER GUIDELINES AND BE INSPIRATIONAL TO THOSE WHO OPEN THEMSELVES TO THE MESSAGE OF BEING, ACCEPTING, AND DOING HUMANNESS. UNDERLYING CLANDESTINE CONSTRUCTS FROM ADLER, FREUD. HORNEY, ROGERS, AND JUNG GIRD THE WICKED WIT AND PRACTICAL COMMUNICATION OF A DELIGHTFUL AND USEFUL BOOK."

JEROLD D. BOZARTH, PH.D.
PROFESSOR EMERITUS
UNIVERSITY OF GEORGIA
AUTHOR, PERSON-CENTERED THERAPY: A REVOLUTIONARY PARADIGM

Why Normal People Do Some Crazy Things:

Nine Fundamentals of Human Behaviors

To Jane,

Everything Tommy tells me about you says that you might love this book — Please enjoy it!

Kevin Davis, M.A.

Publisher's Cataloging In Publication

Davis, Kevin

Why Normal People Do Some Crazy Things /Kevin Davis, M.A.

Includes appendices and index; revised edition, 2010.

LCCN: 2009905061
ISBN-13: 978-0-9819343-0-3

Dedication

This book is dedicated first and foremost to my mother, Doris Davis, an eternal support to my life dreams and the one who never let me give up in life. Without her, I would not be the man I am today. Thanks Mom! I also dedicate this book in memory of my high school English teacher, David Van Etten, who protected my writing style from the other stodgy teachers who he felt would change it. He said, "Your style makes me laugh, so don't let them influence you and say you are too flippant, keep writing your own way." I did.

To my wife, Valerie, who supported this endeavor and kept my doubts at bay. To my first editor, Karen Stone, who took a rough draft and formed it, shaped it, and made it presentable. To Jodi, best selling author, whose simple proximity allowed me to believe I too could write a book. To all my teachers and mentors including Angie, Mo, Brugh, Ram Dass and a host of others too many to name, you have given me the knowledge and self-awareness to write this book.

Finally I dedicate this book to the Mystery which makes my life worth living.

Table of Contents

I have no particular talent. I am passionately inquisitive…

The important thing is not to stop questioning. Curiosity has its own reason for existing. One cannot help but be in awe when he contemplates the mysteries of eternity, of life, of the marvelous structure of reality. It is enough if one tries merely to comprehend a little of this mystery every day…never lose a holy curiosity.

Albert Einstein

Why I Wrote This Book

The field of counseling has been my professional home for twenty years. During this time, I have read many self-help books that have been trendsetters with the "pop psych" culture. My experience has been that most self-help books do not speak broadly about human behavior but rather focus on one particular pattern or problem. These books usually emphasize how to deal with a specific psychological issue or problem, and put less emphasis on explaining or understanding the underlying cause of the problem.

Throughout the years of my clinical practice, the majority of my clients have asked questions about people in their lives who have treated them badly. These questions usually come forward and beg to be answered after the client has been broadsided by some unexpected behavior of a family member, a friend or an associate. Still feeling the sting of the situation, my client asks, "Why would my friend do something like this to ME, my best friend through all these years... and after all we've been through together?" A thousand variations of this theme have spilled from my hurting, confused clients. But no matter how the question is phrased, they desperately seek a context to help them understand the hurtful behavior of others.

Dealing with these kinds of questions, asked so frequently by so many people over the years, sparked my curiosity. I began to approach the understanding of people's behavior in a different way than I had in the early years of my practice. As a young therapist, when a client presented a difficult situation involving another person (for simplicity's sake, let's call the other person the "offending party" or "OP"), I was more concerned with teaching the client to react and respond in an "appropriate" way, and less concerned about helping the client to understand WHY the OP behaved the way he did. As long as my clients responded "appropriately" to these difficult interactions, the reason motivating the OP's behavior seemed irrelevant.

Over time I began to notice a problem with this approach. Though I was successfully teaching my clients to handle conflicts and painful situations, their ongoing relationships with the OPs after the incidents seemed somehow damaged. Without understanding the "why" behind the OPs' behaviors, my clients would emotionally withdraw from them. This withdrawal, while sometimes imperceptible to the OPs, resulted in an unusual distance between them. Over time, I also noticed that some clients began to totally distrust the OP. Their future interactions seemed to be negatively affected by the unspoken sentiment: "If I didn't see that last offense coming, what other unexpected thing could he do to me?"

When I became a Corporate Coach in the early 1990s, the term "coach" was rarely used by anyone outside of a sports arena. As acceptance of the coaching concept grew, I had the unique opportunity to apply my years of psychotherapeutic knowledge and experience to groups of co-workers. Again, I was confronted with more "why" questions, such as, "Why does this employee keep resisting me on this issue?" or "Why are my employees so angry at me when I am just doing my job?" Again, unless the "why" questions were answered to some satisfaction, managers and employees repeatedly distanced from each other, building an intangible wall of distrust, confusion and/or anger. Without genuinely understanding the OPs' behaviors, the wronged co-workers often maintained an emotional and often physical distance, destroying team cohesion and cooperation.

My corporate coaching experiences nudged me into opening my mind to a more holistic approach to the "why" questions posed by my clients.

As a result, over time I adopted a more broad-based perspective, combining an *Overview* perspective, which is focused on understanding the "why" that motivates people's behaviors, and an *Applications* perspective, which is focused on answering the "what" and "how" questions inherent in conflictual, emotionally wounding situations.

In an attempt to help people unravel the mystery behind their difficult interactions with OPs, whether the OP is a loved one, friend or co-worker, I wrote this book to share some of my perspectives about why people behave the way they do. I call these broad categories of motivations that underlie people's actions, "**Fundamentals**" of human behavior.

What are the Fundamentals?

These Fundamentals are simple statements reflecting my perception of the basic motivations behind human behavior. They gelled over time as I worked with clients trying to help them make sense of the unexplainable, crazy, hurtful things people do to each other every day. In developing these Fundamentals, I attempted to categorize large variations of human behavior into simplified, understandable and usable concepts. These concepts are designed to be global enough to cover a wide spectrum of feelings, thoughts, and behaviors and to be relevant to a diverse range of people. I also wanted the concepts to be:

1. applicable to many phases of life,
2. relevant to many life situations,
3. bold in their assertions, and
4. intriguing enough to encourage further thought, self-exploration, and discussion.

These Fundamentals are behavioral one-liners, so to speak, that will hopefully be enlightening and memorable when applied to real-life situations.

Fundamental One
Everyone is terrified and therefore unreliable...until they're not.

Fundamental Two
No one wants you to succeed too well or fail too badly.

Fundamental Three
Genuine interest in and attention to others is a rare commodity.

Fundamental Four
Most relationships, and their recurring problems, are based on power dynamics.

Fundamental Five
Everyone is rushing toward the white picket fence.

Fundamental Six
The Immature Masculine tries to run from or dominate the Feminine.

Fundamental Seven
Everyone points the finger.

Fundamental Eight
We all have multiple personalities.

Fundamental Nine
We are all is addicted to intensity.

Over time, I have observed that each of these Fundamentals holds within it a basic truth or motivation that explains human behavior from several psychological angles: why people act the way they do, as well as why certain conflicts repeatedly arise in people's lives. In fact, **most** of the general questions I have been asked over the years about the motivations underlying the hurtful behavior of the OPs can be answered simply by knowing, understanding and applying these Fundamentals.

We all act in unique ways that make us individuals. Though the wide range of human behaviors often astonishes and confounds us, *generally speaking* (and the whole point of this book is to speak in generalities), I have found that **most** people's early psychological behavior and motivation is governed by these Fundamentals.

What these Fundamentals are not.

These Fundamentals certainly do not hold true for everyone in every situation. In fact, while these Fundamentals will probably ring truer for most of us during early stages of our psychological evolution, they become less true for us as we begin to mature spiritually and psychologically. Does this mean that these Fundamentals primarily apply to children and young adults? In my experience, no. I do not believe that we automatically mature because we age chronologically. In fact, you probably know at least one 'adult' person in your life that rarely exhibits any mature behavior at all!

Yet, no matter what hurdles we may have confronted in our early years, in my experience, life itself seems to push us toward **improving** our inherent natures. This next statement is extremely important to emphasize: The **more** maturity and self confidence we develop psychologically, the **less** these Fundamentals will dictate the way we behave in the world in our daily lives. They will simply be guidelines for understanding others in our lives, and less of a driving force behind our own behaviors.

Ultimately, these Fundamentals are "one man's opinion" and they are intended to serve as a starting point for discussion. Hopefully they will further communication between people who are interested in understanding why people do the crazy, hurtful things they do. They are not meant to shrink the unique differences we have as people, but rather to increase understanding of the enormous complexities that consciously or unconsciously drive our behaviors, thoughts and feelings every day. Once we understand the basic Fundamentals that underlie and motivate our behaviors, we can then begin to open to more mature interactions with people. We can experience life in a different, broader way, one motivated less by fear and more by caring and understanding.

When we no longer live a life unconsciously run by these Fundamentals, our awareness in our relationships and interactions expands. With this expanded perception comes the ability to behave in ways no longer unconsciously driven by Power and Fear. When the shackles of Power and Fear no longer bind us, we can choose to behave and respond differently. As we exercise the power of this choice, we experience the truest human freedom – the ability to share our undefended, authentic self with others.

So let's dig into these Fundamentals to see what we can find out about the behaviors of others…and maybe even understand a little more about our own.

Everyone is terrified and therefore unreliable...until they're not.

Behaviors you might see from OPs include: avoidance behaviors, unexplained unreliability, uncharacteristic or unusual emotional responses, emotional unresponsiveness, acts of greed and selfishness, and most psychologically, physically and emotionally violent acts.

Your senses are heightened and hyper-alert. Your breathing is rapid and shallow. Your sweating palms and brow glisten as you turn your head almost imperceptibly from side to side to pinpoint the threat. Your autonomic response system is in full-blown fight/flight mode. There is no leaping wild animal or speeding car hurdling toward you. Yet, you sense danger. Your outer calm masks an inner terror. To your logical self, you are simply standing in front of your mate as she tells you she is disappointed in you. Your primal self fears annihilation, covers your vulnerability and runs for the emotional hills.

Artist's self description

When you first read this Fundamental, you may think it expresses a very pessimistic attitude about people as a whole. In reality, beneath its seeming negativity is a deeper truth: we are all afraid. Because we are afraid, we do things that are sometimes unusual and many times unexplainable. This is the most important Fundamental of the nine and has earned the number one slot because of its global application to human behavior. Being aware of this single Fundamental can help us to understand the lion's share of people's unusual and inexplicable behavior.

Fundamental One acknowledges that Fear (not the everyday kind, but the instinctive *Fear* attached to survival) is the initial, primary motivating emotion of humans. It is our first line of survival in this huge frightening world of ours. People will unconsciously react to life situations from this fear based foundation **until** they become aware of it and learn to decrease its influence on them.

Think back to recent situations where the actions of a spouse, friend, co-worker, acquaintance, or family member (who we previously dubbed the offending party or "OP") were confusing, "crazy", hurtful or offensive to you. You may have asked yourself one of the following questions, depending on the situation:

Why is my boss/friend/lover acting mean to me?

Why doesn't my partner want to have sex with me?

Why did he/she leave the relationship with no explanation at all?

Why did he/she betray me?

Why did they avoid me when I was in need?

Why don't my married friends call me now that I am single?

Why have my friends pulled away from me just when I met my perfect partner?

Why do they always make fun of me?

Your best chance to understand the answer to such questions is to ask: "What frightened or scared the OP?" or "What is the OP afraid of?" or "What could the OP possibly be defending against?"

Yet, be forewarned. Often, we don't have enough inside information to satisfactorily figure out the specific fear motivating the OP's behavior. Many times even the OP does not know what is motivating them. I genuinely believe that **at least** 90% of violent interactions are the result of conscious or unconscious fear. Yet, when OP's are probed, they often offer some knee-jerk response as to why they acted (or reacted) the way they did. How then do we begin to understand what emotions motivate people when people themselves are often not aware of their motivations?

The easiest time to learn about people's fundamental psychology is to observe children. From infancy to our early teens, our emotions are often so raw, close to the surface and felt so purely that we lack the capacity to hide them very well. Because our feelings are so easily observable when we are younger, it seemed our parents were able to magically read our minds and our moods. Most parents who pay attention to their children know when their offspring are happy or sad, frustrated or bored, and, most especially, when they are angry or scared. Their emotions are often an open book that can be read at any given moment.

It is only later in life that we begin to develop our ability to hide our emotions from others. In difficult situations, we often hide them from ourselves. Unfortunately, hiding our emotions eventually causes more problems than it solves. Hiding our emotions from others, may initially feel safer. Over time though, if we do this too effectively or too often, we corrode our relationships with others. Even worse, when we try to hide our feelings from ourselves, we corrode our Soul.

Our willingness to display our emotions may change as we get older. The existence of the emotions themselves does not. What motivates us when we are younger is often what motivates us when we are adults. This is why therapists so often ask the seemingly trite question, "Tell me about your childhood," in early counseling sessions.

While everyone most assuredly gets chronologically older, not everyone matures spiritually and psychologically. Because of this, Fundamental One exerts influence throughout the span of most people's lives. In fact, Fear is so influential in many people's lives that it determines their every emotional decision—and, thus, their behaviors.

When I was in my early teens, I used to feel that I was the only one in the world who had fears because everyone else seemed to be so together and cool. No one ever let on (at least to me) that they were scared of anything. I felt as if I lived alone in an internally terrified world. My thin shoulders seemed to carry the weight of enough fears for everyone.

When I was a freshman in High School, I had a whole host of fears that now seem ridiculous. Teenagers, in case you do not remember, have a primary fear that stands out above all others—embarrassment. They are so certain they will be devastated by feeling embarrassed that they avoid any situation that could possibly expose them to it. During my early teens, my list of fears included: eating alone at a table in the school cafeteria, standing in the school hallway alone without a pack of friends with which to huddle, dancing at a party, or going to a party or movie alone. At that age, going anywhere by yourself meant you were a loser. Going to new places, meeting new people, not having a date to social gatherings—I never heard anyone else admit to being fearful about these situations. But they were devastating to me.

I tried to protect myself by dealing with my fears as my peers did: I pretended they did not exist. Most of the time I simply avoided uncomfortable situations altogether. This technique worked just fine until someone else insisted on doing something I did not want to do, which unfortunately happened more often than I preferred. Each time I did something uncomfortable, I felt, looked, and acted awkward in front of other people, which caused (Oh my God) embarrassment. We teenagers hated embarrassment. Because of this, we, me included, did some crazy things.

One of the first times I consciously experienced someone's crazy behavior was in the eighth grade. I was standing in the school cafeteria lunch line with a friend of mine, waiting to get our food. I asked him a question about "why" he had done something (I can't remember the specifics). WHAM! A split second later, I was doubled over. He had hauled off and punched me extremely hard in the stomach, a totally unexpected reaction! I was shocked—and in pain. My mind was working quickly, trying to make sense of this hurtful betrayal. Why would he hit me simply for asking a question?

A plausible answer came to me years later: he was scared. Something about my question threatened him. His reaction was to fight rather than take flight. The "punch from nowhere" looked like some crazy, unexplainable act. In reality, it was an automatic, defensive response meant to protect a vulnerable spot in my friend's psyche.

This example stands out in my mind because it was the first seemingly totally "off the wall" behavior I experienced from a friend. Its impact was so strong and my awareness was so heightened that, in self-defense I began to notice when other people did unexplained, crazy things. I did not want to be blind-sided again. Years later, when I began to make some sense of this event, I realized it was my very tangible introduction to fear-motivated behavior.

Author's personal experience

Twenty years later, as a psychotherapist, I listen daily to stories of how people feel about different interactions in their lives. It is absolutely enlightening. I have been oddly comforted by realizing that everyone experiences fears throughout their lives. In fact, many people are more fearful than I am. The bravest people I run across - even heroes in the community—have admitted privately that they were terrified while doing their heroic or brave feat.

Over the years as I listened to my clients' stories, I began seeing the world in a new way and I began tactfully questioning people about how they handled fearful situations. From their answers, I began to see a pattern: no matter what area of challenge we discussed, my clients consistently chose the **least fearful** path they could find for themselves, given all the options before them. They discarded "fear provoking" paths or unfamiliar solutions, simply labeling them as "inferior", "incorrect" or just plain "bad." Instead, they chose "tried-and-true" alternatives that generally produced predictable results.

My cafeteria-line friend could have reacted to my question in a number of different ways. He could have told me to "shut up" (verbal), ignored my question (non-verbal) or walked away (avoidance/flight). But he chose to respond automatically with a punch (fight), and it definitely produced a predictable result - I stopped questioning.

My new awareness with my clients also expanded my perspective in social situations. Whenever people around me describe how they hate someone or something, or when they insult someone or something, by looking behind their words I usually discover that there is an underlying discomfort (fear) they feel around such people, places or events. I no longer see bigots and bullies simply as evil, frightening monsters. They are, more accurately, frightened, immature people. Those we label as critical people, angry people, mean people, controlling people, rigid people, revolutionaries, rebels, gang members, and even snobs are all driven by a fundamental fear-based nature. I have observed that most of their aggressive behavior is based on this dynamic: when taken out of their safety zone, or confronted by a situation they perceive as threatening, they become terrified and take aggressive action that serves one primary objective: fear reduction.

Psychotherapists call this behavior "compensation." For example, people use aggressive behaviors to compensate for the fear they experience in social or relationship situations. Rather than simply experiencing the feeling of vulnerability, which frightens them, they criticize, strike out physically, and/or hurl insults or judgments at others to make themselves feel more powerful (safer) in the moment.

Other emotional behaviors are also born out of fear. Anger immediately comes to mind because of the fight or flight nature of anger (primal fear). Arrogance is a little harder to recognize because its outward behavior appears primarily dismissive; but it is still simply Fear. Its deepest roots seem to mirror the ostrich's behavior of sticking its head in the sand when it is scared. "I am scared so I will ignore you, pretend you do not exist, or in some way remove you from my attention." This can take the form of a dismissive gesture, an insult, or some verbal condescending remark; but it is nonetheless still motivated by Fear.

Jealousy is another emotion born out of fear—specifically the fear of scarcity and loss. We are only jealous when we are afraid that someone else has something that we do not have or may never get, or when we fear that someone can take away something we value and don't want to lose.

Theft also has its basis in fear of scarcity. If people did not fear a lack of something, there would be no reason to steal. Greed is also on the list of fear-driven emotions. We only feel the "need" to hoard if we are afraid of not having "enough." It is also interesting to note that many of the so-called "seven deadly sins" are directly related to the underlying emotion of Fear.

The effect of Fear is not just relegated to the world of the common man. We also see it raise its emotionally powerful head in environments where conscious, aware, trained people are present. For example, one of the negative byproducts of the pervasive fear underlying Fundamental One is a group etiquette phenomenon that I call the "tyranny of the child." This dynamic shows up in self-help and other interactive groups. It comes into play when one member of a group tries to change the topic or flow of a group discussion when they become uncomfortable (fearful). The triggered person speaks up and demands a change in the group behavior or topic to suit his or her own level of comfort.

Let's say the topic of sex comes up in a discussion and that someone in the group does not want to discuss sex at all. The triggered person usually demands that the topic be changed by using labels such as "inappropriate" or "offensive" to camouflage the mere fact that they are fearful of the topic. Looking at the dynamic from a group perspective, we see that one person becomes "offended" by a topic and shuts down what might be an otherwise important or beneficial adult discussion for the group as a whole.

The "tyranny of the child" scenario says that it is "politically correct" for the group to stop its interaction or work if anyone is "offended" so that the group can address the offended person's wishes. As a result, the most emotionally fragile member of the group is catered to, like a child, at the expense of other more mature adult interactions. The adult who is emotionally weakest "wins" control of the group.

What differentiates "tyranny" from simple feedback is the accompanying demand. If someone simply shares their discomfort about a topic without demanding a topic change, that person is simply stating the emotional impact of that topic on them. Doing so without demanding a change actually builds intimacy and promotes a deeper discussion on a feeling level.

In summary, it is a positive act to share the emotional impact of a specific topic or event. On the other hand, using this impact to demand a change in topics based on a "moral high ground" that a topic is "offensive" or "inappropriate" is most often a manipulation used to avoid feeling discomfort and, ultimately, facing one's fears. Over-sensitivity is often simply another expression of self-centeredness and is thus a childlike emotion that expresses a need for the person's wishes to be the center of the group's interaction.

As my experience with individuals and groups grew over the years, I formulated what I thought was an inevitable and logical conclusion:

The root of all evil is FEAR

and

we all have way too much of it.

Because everyone is full of Fear, actually terrified in my estimation, we do things all the time in personal and business settings that hurt other people. For example, in the normal course of business, partners steal credit from you, co-workers unjustly let you take the blame for a failed idea, or companies harass people who ask threatening questions or stand up to authority. These "out-of-the-blue" hurtful and unfair behaviors are primarily the offspring of Fear.

To recap, in all areas of interaction, Fear is the primary emotional driver in most people's lives. In an attempt to protect ourselves from what we perceive to be fearful situations, people will do unusual, unexpected and sometimes hurtful things.

Fear Makes Us Unreliable…

Fear, I believe, also makes people generally unreliable. In pondering Fundamental One, I realized that many of the "why" questions asked by clients and friends were attempts to handle the disappointment they feel when someone they relied on (or wanted to rely on) has shown themselves to be unreliable. This is especially true of interactions between friends. We may be miffed at the cable guy for not showing up when he said he would, but we are devastated when our "best" friend betrays us. We are somewhat upset when a ride shows up late, but we are beside ourselves when a friend doesn't speak up in our defense when someone is cruel or insulting to us. We are disappointed when a friend doesn't pitch in enough when we need them, but we are crushed when they totally turn their back on us when we are most in need or alone. If we look behind our hurt and disappointment in these situations, we can see that it is usually some form of Fear that made our friend unreliable.

We are, for example, unreliable when we do not come to a friend's defense because we fear some consequence. We are unreliable when we avoid former work mates who were fired because it might look bad to be seen with them. We are unreliable when we do not say something difficult to a friend because we are afraid they might get mad. We are unreliable when someone shouts for help, and we walk the other way to avoid conflict. We are unreliable when, in order to avoid the ugliness of a situation, we turn a blind eye to atrocities in the world when we could help.

Fear, then, ultimately forces us to distance ourselves from one another. The beginning of the movie *Jerry Maguire* vividly shows this behavior in action. Jerry, a leading sports agent played by Tom Cruise, is caught up in a moment of inspiration and puts into writing his philosophy expressing the need to care about clients in his business.

In response, and before the ink was barely dry, he was ostracized and thrown out of his company by the same people he trained and worked with for years. His kind of thinking was too far out of the comfortable box of their concept of doing business. Because his thinking expressed a vulnerability and sensitivity that was foreign to his associates, "they" had to get rid of him to avoid the discomfort produced by his way of thinking. They did not want to entertain the possibility of changing their own thinking and behavior. Why experience vulnerability when you can just remove the source of the discomfort?

This inherent desire to remove uncomfortable (and therefore dangerous) objects is so basic to survival that it is actually a part of every human's physiology. Psychological survival tactics are mirrored by the human immune system. When it encounters a potentially foreign object in the body, it metaphorically asks the simple question: "Is this me or not me?" meaning "Is this a part of my body or something foreign (dangerous/irritating) to my body?" If the answer is "not me," our immune system attacks the foreign body with the intent to eliminate the "enemy." Organizations and individuals are essentially similar to the immune system in their response to outsiders or outside thinking. They identify foreign thoughts or persons and destroy them if possible because they are seen as a threat or irritant.

"This story is hard to convey because when I was there I could see his face and feel the emotion so well, but here goes...

My present boss and I grew up together as kids and technically he's not my boss, but we like to play with titles, and we are just the best of friends. All of our lives he has been like Spock from Star Trek, almost emotionless except for the occasional chuckle or smile. I know he feels, he just doesn't show it. So one time we hadn't seen each other in forever...it was like three weeks I was out of town or something, and I walk into his building to see him in his office.

I had a little anticipation; you know the excitement between friends when you haven't seen each other in a while, that kinda SURPRISE kinda feeling? You know...(laughs)...Yes it can happen between guys too!

So I haven't seen him, and I'm about to unexpectedly drop by his office when I see this new guy he's recently hired sitting in his office talking to him. They seem to be just talking casually so I go on in.

He looks up and sees me and you can just see his face light up with surprise and this HUGE smile comes over his face like, 'Well, well, well, looky who the cat drug in'. I see I've pleasantly surprised him and I light up myself with a big smile, you know, nothing Gay or anything, we just haven't seen each other in a while and all this happened in a flash of a second.

He then glances at his new employee, I mean split second like, as if he might have been caught looking excited or pleased or something by the new guy. Realizing this possibility, his face just DROPS—total shift—and he practically shouts at me, 'What are you doing here? Can't you see I'm in an important meeting! What are you wearing…a casual shirt, you should have on a dress shirt, and what is that…no belt…what is this!' in this nasty, nasty raised tone.

The new employee practically jumps out of his seat from the obvious shift in tone. Anger, pure anger. I hadn't made it two steps into the office before he is yelling at me. I figure any second he's going to stop and say, 'Gotcha', or something and laughingly ask me where I've been all this time. But NOOOOOOO, he keeps pouring it on. I can't even remember what he said at that point I was so uncomfortable by it all as was the new guy sitting in front of him. It obviously had no connection to the reality of the moment and it just creeped me out…I mean REALLY creeped me out.

I looked down at the new guy and said softly, 'He isn't usually like this,' and turned on my heels and walked out. 'Good,' my friend said loudly. 'Good, leave!'

The whole thing was so weird and freaky that right as I left his office I got a hit on what had happened. I can't prove anything but I really believe that he was so overwhelmed by his happiness to see me that he got scared. Scared from the sheer intensity of his emotions and the vulnerability of feeling that in front of a new employee. But like a little kid who has feelings for a girl, he punched me (verbally) instead. We never talked about it, of course."

From actual conversation

...until we're not.

"Until we're not," means there is hope. There is light at the end of some people's Fear tunnel. There are people in the world who have overcome their fundamental fears to the point that they are no longer unreliable. They have moved beyond their primal fears to the point where they have become trustworthy. "Until we're not" means there is a way out of the slavery of Fear. But let's not get ahead of ourselves....

This first Fundamental is perhaps the hardest of all the Fundamentals to accept. When you think through its assumptions, you will start to see how far and wide the reach of Fear is in our lives. You may start to question whether there is any negative feeling or behavior that is not ultimately born from Fear. This is a heavy thought. And, what do we do with it? We certainly don't live in a world where we can eliminate Fear from our emotional make-up.

So why would I choose such a seemingly depressing beginning for my Fundamentals? The reason is a personal one. I find it liberating to simplify much of human motivation to such a primary emotion. While Fundamental One may seem disturbing at first glance, think about several examples of people's negative behaviors from your own life. Does Fundamental One give you a new perspective in understanding why someone acted the way they did in the past? Well, it did for me.

Understanding Fundamental One moved me into a place of feeling compassion toward the OPs in my life. Recognizing the power and pervasiveness of Fear as a motivator gave me my first comforting insight into the emotion behind people's behavior. This then became the first layer of the foundation from which I could forgive them. I find it harder to forgive what I cannot understand, and as far reaching as Fundamental One may seem, believing it, and applying it, has allowed me to forgive people's behavior in ways I never imagined.

"Oh, they must **really** have been scared to have done that," has become a mantra for me. At times, it soothes me. It doesn't take away the pain of the transgression, but it softens my initial anger and hurt.

It will always be painful when friends are unreliable. And I regret those times in the past when my own unreliability has hurt others. Because I understand the powerful emotions behind Fundamental One, I don't hold grudges for long anymore and I don't hide from people as deeply in my defenses as I used to.

So how can we best use the awareness and knowledge that Fundamental One offers us? Simply put, if we know everyone is terrified, then many of our interactions with people will invariably take that fact into account. Armed with this knowledge, we can approach interactions with others with a new found awareness and consciousness that offers us an alternative reaction. Rather than putting up our guard and running into the defensive mode of blaming and attacking, we can choose to respond differently—with curiosity and gentleness.

When I was younger, I had a habit of ignoring people in social situations. I generally didn't ignore what they said—I ignored their "social needs". I assumed everyone around me needed nothing from me to feel comfortable. I assumed people were totally self-contained, confident and fearless. I worked hard to maintain my own emotional independence and expected everyone else to do the same.

I would walk through a party, gathering or casual get-together speaking only to those attendees that intrigued me, without acknowledging anyone else. An interesting artifact of that period is that, using this interaction style, I could invariably anger 50% of the people in any given room I entered without ever having said a word to most of them. I could not figure out why they were angry since I had not spoken to them at all. Eventually I realized this was the point—-I did not acknowledge them in the slightest.

In retrospect, I know a high percentage of those I angered at past gatherings would have been fine if I had just given them some acknowledgement. As the years have gone by and I have had the opportunity to look back with a new perspective, I understand people I overlooked felt I was dismissive of them. Unknowingly I was. They saw me as arrogant, snobby, and cliquish —-perceptions to which I had no idea I had contributed.

Author's personal experience

This personal example illustrates how understanding Fundamental One has impacted my relationships. Before I understood this Fundamental, I interacted with people based on my assumption that they were confident, emotionally sturdy and needed nothing from me to feel "safe". Now I realize that, underlying the simple desire for fun and affiliation, most people's initial interactions are ultimately a test to see if others are safe or not. Most people, of course, would never admit to this need for social safety. When meeting new people, they may say they need to "find something in common" or see if the person is "interesting." Whether they acknowledge it or not, a person's comfort level with a new person is a huge part of the decision to interact again.

I am increasingly aware of my body posture, my tone of voice, my conversation volume, and a whole host of behaviors that affect how "safe" I am for people to be around. Most people are not even conscious that they monitor these types of non-verbal cues in others. But people quickly judge others as "safe" or "unsafe" based on these cues. We label people we choose not to socialize with to justify our unconscious reactions. "Obnoxious", "pushy", "rude", "too quiet", "too loud", are only a few reasons we give when we write someone off our social list. But, no matter what words we use, they all speak to a feeling of being uncomfortable (fearful/unsafe) when we are around that person.

Understanding this Fundamental encourages me to walk through the world in a proactive way that at least attempts to provide a safe environment for those around me. How do I do this? Simply acknowledging others initially increases the ease of interaction. A thoughtful, curious question about someone's life, a simple smile or a wave acknowledges the other person and addresses people's need to be "seen" by those around them. Any other further acts of interest are simply gravy (author's note: gravy is a good thing). Through a few simple acts of acknowledgement, one can avoid hundreds of forms of entanglements, jealousy, resentment, anger, and just plain ill will. Every action done with the intent of increasing social safety decreases social fear and, thus, brings an ease and efficiency to our interactions.

At first, it may seem that becoming aware of and attending to people's fundamental fear requires a lot of work. It can at first, but the pay offs are big if you do. The negative price you pay is high if you do **not**. Adding a little conscious attention to our interactions with others easily lessens the negative consequences of Fundamental One. Even the smallest of efforts can greatly increase efficiency and flow in social interactions, which are hampered by the fundamental social fears we all carry throughout our lives.

As described above, behavior in casual social settings can change when we simply pay attention to and acknowledge those around us. But what value does attentive behavior have in a circle of emotionally close friends? In my observation, these close circles are extremely rare, but within them, any extra attentiveness given to those within the group boosts emotional intimacy between members to a higher level than previously experienced within that group. As intimacy grows, so does the confidence and closeness between members. Acknowledging people who are close to you is never a wasted effort, even when it might seem unnecessary.

The last application of this Fundamental is the most important application of all. I said in the beginning of this chapter that I made "Everyone is terrified" the first Fundamental because of its far-reaching effects on people's lives. While I have discussed Fundamental One's effect on the individual, it must also be understood on a more global scale. On an individual scale, the Fear inherent in Fundamental One usually only affects the immediate circle of people around the person experiencing it. What happens, though, when a political leader wants to use the power of Fundamental One? On a global scale, it could be used to change, manipulate, or influence an entire country or region of the globe. Put simply, Fundamental One is so influential in people's lives that it has been used by leaders throughout history to further political agendas, good and evil.

Can you think of any political leaders throughout history that have used the fact that people are terrified to get their agendas accepted?

How about Hitler in the 1940's? He is probably one of the better-known examples of a leader who manipulated through Fear. Listen to what his minister of propaganda, Hermann Goering, said in an interview about manipulating people to do one's bidding:

"Naturally, the common people don't want war, neither in Russia nor in England nor in America, nor for that matter in Germany. That is understood. But, after all, it is the leaders of the country who determine the policy and it is always a simple matter to drag the people along, whether it is a democracy, a fascist dictatorship, or a Parliament or a Communist dictatorship."

"There is one difference," (the interviewer) pointed out. "In a democracy the people have some say in the matter through their elected representatives, and in the United States only Congress can declare wars."

"Oh, that is all well and good, but, voice or no voice, the people can always be brought to the bidding of the leaders. That is easy. All you have to do is tell them they are being attacked and denounce the pacifists for lack of patriotism and exposing the country to danger. It works the same way in any country."

Hermann Goering

The ability to influence an entire country using the primary emotion of Fear underscores the tremendous power behind Fundamental One. It could be argued that Fundamental One was used by President Roosevelt to get a reluctant United States to join the fight against Hitler in W.W. II. Roosevelt's use of Fundamental One would arguably be for the cause of Good. Hitler's propaganda machine using Fundamental One—not so much. See if you can think of any other leaders throughout history who have used this Fundamental to manipulate their country's people.

To most effectively apply the wisdom of Fundamental One, at the global or individual level, assume humans are inherently emotionally fragile, and you cannot go wrong. Even if you encounter someone who seems truly fearless on the outside, your attentiveness or safety building actions will not be wasted. While it is not our duty to try to fix or soothe the fears of everyone around us, you can attempt to avoid throwing gasoline on the fear fire that smolders in each of us.

So here we are at the end of the first Fundamental. Are you feeling wiser, more aware and more compassionate toward the OPs in your life? Or are you feeling manipulated, a bit angry, or even (dare I say) fearful? Sometimes thinking that we live in a world where people are primarily motivated by Fear can feel overwhelming. Well, fear not. You have taken the first step toward understanding the hurtful behaviors of those around you. And you might even be feeling a little kinder toward yourself.

We are all, and I do mean all, (and this includes you) dealing with rational and irrational fears and they greatly influence our behaviors for most of our lives. Just knowing this can begin to influence the way we react to others' behaviors. It may even spark a new interest in our own.

No one wants you to succeed too well or fail too badly.

> Behaviors you might see from OPs include: avoidance behaviors or pronounced lack of interest; hurtful gossip/rumors circulated by previously trusted friends/co-workers; acts of betrayal; acts of psychological sabotage.

In 1993, I had the good fortune to be a part of a "corporate culture change" experiment in Britain involving a large multi-national corporation. Two other corporate coaches and I had been looking for an opportunity to use the principles of Group Dynamics in a business setting. We reasoned that if we could put team members into a group setting where they felt comfortable enough to actually talk about their problems with each other, they would work more cohesively as a team. This seems obvious when you think about it. Yet, this principle is rarely used by major corporate consulting firms because the technique is seen as being too psychologically threatening to the participants. Because the method had not been "tried and proven true," those who were comfortable with the status quo were too scared to practice it (see Fundamental One).

This corporation had decided to step outside the box. Management voted to undertake a daring, never before attempted, overhaul of their upper management tiers. Simply stated, their goal was to move from an overly bureaucratic, hierarchically layered management style to a more flexible and cooperative team management approach—in short, to change the very foundation of their corporate culture. To accomplish this, they planned to hire a group of corporate coaches with a fresh approach to team building. I was one of these coaching professionals. We were given the task of developing and applying the method to be used to "team build" the management levels. Knowing that we were about to use a radical approach never before seen by this company (or many others); we emphasized our low cost and the fact that we offered a fresh consulting approach. "You've tried everyone else in the world (literally), now try us" was our sales tactic.

I tell you all this to emphasize the "gutsy" nature of what we were about to attempt. Everyone inside the company understood the high stakes involved in implementing our radical approach. The unorthodox nature of our experiment also caught the interest of my personal and professional friends at home. Here I was, a thirty-three-year old "novice" coach, temporarily moving to the U.K. to try a radical team building approach with one of the more influential companies in the world! In my excitement, I organized a send off party for myself and invited all my friends and colleagues. Throwing a party to celebrate my newfound opportunity sounded fantastically fun.

It wasn't.

Outside of maybe three close friends, the other attendees took one giant step back from me. I was stumped. At face value, it seemed obvious that we should all be celebrating. I had gotten a **huge** career break and the opportunity to do cutting-edge, experimental work that also carried the further status-raising mystique of being "international." Yet, at the ill-fated party, people smiled politely when I told them what I was doing. Their interest and congratulations felt forced. I ignored this at first, but as the "forced smile" syndrome spread through the room to the outer layers of my peers and professional associates, I became disappointed and confused. Why was this happening? Was this not a happy occasion? In the rush of packing and moving and planning the curriculum, I tabled my curiosity about what I felt was an "unexplainable reaction" until another day.

Jump to a year later. After the unbelievably successful coaching venture in Britain, in which our experiment worked well beyond our wildest dreams, I came back ready to apply the same techniques to American companies and to continue my brilliant success here!

I was welcomed back with the emotional equivalent of a smattering of applause.

Stateside, my success from across the pond was short lived. Within a few months, my professional success train hit a brick wall. No doors were opening. No calls were being returned. "Home run" possibilities were turning into strikeouts. Several months went by. Not one potential client would commit to even a trial run. I began to question the merits of the program I had personally experienced as producing phenomenal results. Maybe the whole technique of employees talking to each other in a circle was just too threatening after all.

With all of my marketing efforts focused entirely on the coaching aspect of my career and not my therapeutic practice, I was quickly going broke. As it became more and more obvious to those around me that my initial coaching success was not going to be replicated, a funny thing happened: Friends who were hearing the grapevine news of my potential demise started contacting me again. They offered help and gave me leads to get my foot in the door with companies I had not been able to crack. Suddenly, it seemed everyone wanted to help me get back on the success train I had ridden over from Britain. The world looked brighter. All of my old "friends" and colleagues were back by my side, cheering me on.

Even with new coaching possibilities brewing, I still needed a source of more immediate income to pay my bills. I began focusing more on my private practice and began seeing psychotherapy clients again. But my lifestyle (and the resulting bills) had grown beyond my short-term marketing capability. I decided to work weekends in our family cleaning business to make immediate cash while my coaching business grew.

At the time, this seemed to be, simply, a wise, practical decision. No great fortunes to be made here, but the work would pay the majority of my bills while I continued to promote my coaching business. No big deal, I thought.

Wrong, again.

You see, my stopgap job unfortunately carried with it a title that made people unbelievably uncomfortable. Family business or not, I was now a JANITOR (insert frightening music and horrified screams here). I may have been the only Masters level, internationally experienced Corporate Coach/Psychotherapist JANITOR in the world, but to everyone I knew I was now simply a JANITOR (insert frightening music and horrified screams here). Although I genuinely enjoyed both the work and my co-workers, I was aware that very few people would understand why, if I was such a hotshot corporate coach, I was working as a JANITOR. Forget that it was a family business, that I knew the management personally, and that I worked only on weekends. Forget that I was probably the highest paid janitor in the world and I was helping turn a basically unprofitable business into a lean, mean, profitable, cleaning machine. Nope. To the rest of the world, I was now a certified LOSER (insert lowered eyes and hushed voices here).

It only took a few months for the "friends" who had returned to my side to start falling back away. Ironically, I learned the hard way that people don't mind helping out a starving corporate coach for a while - - but they hate even socializing with a working janitor. My previously envious professional peers took untold glee in my new job title of "Janitor" and they spread the news of my "down trodden" state around the mental health field like a firestorm. Gossip continued, stories were embellished, my demise was greatly exaggerated. The few friends I saw socially during this time looked down at the floor and suffered through uncomfortable silences when I told them how much I loved working as a janitor, which I truly did. "No, really, it's a HOOT", I'd tell them.

"I'm sure, Kevin," they'd say with pity in their voices.

I just laughed.

So there it was - the infamous rags to riches to rags story all in a period of about three years. When I was climbing to the top, I was everyone's best friend. We are all striving upward and we feel good when we are a part of someone's success. But, when I was truly on top for a time, many friends disappeared. People were only willing to celebrate my success to the level they believed that they, too, could achieve. But sometimes when success sits at the top of a hill that they believe they cannot climb themselves, they back away from the challenge. (I had "succeeded too well.") When I was heading back down the hill, people showed up again because they felt we were back on more equal footing. When I began heading WAY down, they backed up and left again. Now I was a loser. And no one wants to be friends with a loser. (I had "failed too badly.") The trained observer of behavior in me watched people's reactions to my career highs and lows with curiosity. My experience of the comings and goings of my friends later gelled into my simple statement of Fundamental Two.

Famous people know the ups and downs of Fundamental Two all too well. Hollywood is ground zero for it. Movie stars and celebrities live the Fundamental Two experience over and over as their careers vacillate. Stars often describe the phenomenon with an off-handed comment made during interviews, which are usually given following recent movie or project successes. "Well, let's just say people are returning my phone calls again," they say, while laughing. They know all too well that people's loyalties are influenced both negatively and positively by their career success - or lack thereof. An often-repeated one-liner equates the size of a T.V. star's post-show party with the show's Nielson ratings - the higher the rating, the larger the crowd. When the ratings go down, so do the post party attendance numbers.

Those of us that have not made it to the silver screen are not exempt from the relationship ebb and flow inherent in Fundamental Two behaviors. Receive an unexpected inheritance, win a lottery, or move away into a luxurious house in an expensive neighborhood and see what happens. In the aftermath of any unexpected windfall that increases your social or financial status, your relationships will shift. (People don't want you to succeed too well.)

"So we are sitting there at O'Malley's, me, Johnny, his girlfriend and my girlfriend at the time drinking pitchers, this is like sophomore, undergraduate year. I'm 19 or 20 or something and we are celebrating Johnny having been filmed in a part in a movie. He's like my closest friend at the time and he just finished his last shot of the film. It starred the Landry twins who were the sexy vixens of the time. He actually had a fight scene with the main character. My friend...on camera...he's a movie star to us!

Just three months earlier this guy is crying on his bed because he lost a job opportunity that he thought would have been perfect for him. He's like WAILING about 'what am I going to do now my life is over...there is nothing for me out there now...there is no way I will ever get a decent job now!' You know the kind of 20's angst and drama we all had at some time, and I'm dying myself because, being 20 something also, I am sure he is not exaggerating his situation in the least. Three months ago I am praying, no yelling, for God to give this guy a break, anything to make him feel better.

What happens? He gets a movie part, **total fluke!**

His first movie part, he's on camera, we're all toasting his inevitable movie career, and I'm sitting there pissed as hell. My **friend**, and I'm still pissed as hell. Oh yea, I'm toasting him, truly genuine toasts...'to a long movie career...next stop Hollywood and kissing scenes with Farrah Fawcett!' Yeaaaa! But I am still jealous beyond my wildest imaginations. I don't want to be, but I am. Norman Mailer said, "Every time a friend of mine succeeds, a little part of me dies.' I agree with him."

From actual conversation

Lose social or financial status and the second assumption of Fundamental Two (people don't want you to fail too badly) kicks in. Often when there is a loss (or a potential loss), loyalty issues with friends will appear. When there is a loss of reputation, job, money, spouse or partner (or anything that brings up discomfort or fear in others) friends may begin to fall away unexpectedly. Or, conversely, friends may not come to your side to offer support or 'defend' you against others' insults. Illness or loss of health is another area where

Fundamental Two can apply. Have you ever wondered why some people visit you or a loved one in the hospital and others avoid you when you have had an accident or during an illness? You may have heard an excuse similar to: "I didn't want to see you/him/her in that condition. It makes me sad/uncomfortable." Sometimes this common excuse is genuine (this would fall under Fundamental One… "People are terrified") and, at other times it is just an excuse for laziness or disinterest.

Oddly, Fundamental Two behavior can also appear in situations that involve pregnancy or the birth of a child. For example, in groups of younger professionals when several friends are "trying to get pregnant" at the same time, if one woman becomes pregnant more quickly and easily than the others, behavior catalyzed by the "success" side of Fundamental Two may show up. Unfortunately, the tragedy of the death of a child may cause a powerful reaction that may look similar to a Fundamental Two "failure" response. In both these circumstances, friends, and in some instances, loved ones, may unexplainably, and sadly, disappear.

In the business setting, Fundamental Two behavior can be set off by a promotion or an upward job transfer, or a demotion or a downward job transfer. A significant bonus given to only one employee or to a few executives, a firing or a downsizing can also set off a Fundamental Two reaction.

When someone leaves the corporate world to start their own business, a strange mix of emotions may show up in the circle of co-workers one leaves behind—a sort of simultaneous Fundamental Two expression of "Gosh, I hope they make it because I really like them," quickly followed by, "but if they succeed, I will just die."

Emotions run to the two extremes because many people have a secret fantasy of being their own boss and "making it on their own." They are usually just too scared to try. On one hand, they want to hang around to see if you succeed, proving that maybe they can succeed, too. But, because they may have an unconscious, adverse reaction to being shown by someone else that a person can be successful outside of corporate America, they would be just as fine if you failed. In fact, they can exhale if you do fail, because it validates their own fear of trying to start a business themselves. If you totally fail, you will rarely hear from your old co-workers again. Subconsciously, they may not want to witness your failure, because this might pour water on their own barely smoldering dream.

Authors, especially first time authors, are often shocked at the reactions of peers, friends and often their families, following the publication of their first book. Many of the people close to them will never read the book—even if it is given to them for free! If they do read it, they might make vague comments about it, such as, "Well, you sure had a lot to say" or "Gosh, that was some book." Assuming the material is of some reasonable quality, these are often the comments of the envious, who feel their own life story—the one they may never have the courage to write—should have been published instead of yours. "Who do you think YOU are to be writing a book?" is a common, unexpressed sentiment. It seems to run parallel to feelings of co-workers toward someone who ventures out on their own. Writing a book is often seen as entrepreneurial, even though it may not have been written for the purpose of starting a business. Doing any new venture without a safety net evokes great fear in people (see Fundamental One). Such actions are generally seen as blazing a heroic trail into the unknown. And while fantasies of expressing ourselves and being brave enough to conquer the unknown live inside almost all of us, most of us lack the courage to attempt it. In fact, we often end up resenting those who do have the courage to actually give their dreams a try.

So, some of us go back to the ostrich technique we may have mastered as a response to Fear. We stick our heads in the sand and ignore that others might be more courageous than we are. We don't want to witness their brave moves because it shows us that we are most likely more afraid than they are. Rather than deal with these internal issues, we ignore them. Over time, we get better and better at ignoring people who push our "issue buttons." With practice, we might stop caring about other people altogether. Why pay attention to others or care about what they are doing or feeling when it might bring up a painful comparison?

For insight into this question, let's turn to the next Fundamental.

FUNDAMENTAL THREE

Genuine interest in and attention to Others is a rare commodity.

> Behaviors you might see from OPs include: behaviors of condescension, ignoring, or indifference; short attention span/disinterested when listening to others; allowing cell phones to ring during theatrical events; repeated/prolonged cellphone use or texting in personal, social situations.

Growing up, except for the few of us who enjoyed being obstinate, we all said "please" and "thank you" without too much of a fight. Even as children we instinctively felt it was not only a correct thing to do—it was also a good thing to do. We didn't hate being well mannered. We just hated being told by adults what to do and say in front of other people—especially our friends. To increase the potential for social embarrassment in the South in the sixties, it wasn't only our parents who told us how to act. Any adult witnessing a transgression had the socially sanctioned right to correct us. In the South we were, to use Hillary Clinton's phrase, a village. Everyone within shouting range took responsibility for everyone's children and how they behaved. In addition, part of my rearing included schooling in the social niceties we called "manners". My siblings and I were drilled in the "appropriate and expected behaviors" throughout our youth. "Sayy pleeeeeeeeease," was a mantra heard throughout every southern boy's and girl's childhood. It was matched in frequency only by the refrain: "Now sayy thank yooooooou." You knew you were growing up when you got to witness children younger than you wrestle with their embarrassment at being reminded to "mind your manners" by adults. The rite of passage was complete when you started saying the polite phrases without the prompting of an adult, indicating that you had been appropriately socialized. You knew by that time that you would soon be old enough to start hounding children younger than you to "say Pleeeaaaase."

On top of the appropriate and frequent use of "plcaeeeease" and "thank yoooooooooooou", there was a broad and detailed code of behavior. It covered practically everything: burping (say "excuse me" if it happens), cursing (never do it), attending to a friend's needs (always offer), and how to address adults with respect ("Sir" and "Ma'am"), to name a few. All these actions fell into the "manners" category. All manners, with the possible exception of which silverware to use, were geared toward making those around you feel acknowledged and comfortable.

Those who mastered the Southern values of graciousness and appropriate behaviors were given the much-respected designation of "having good manners." Socially minded people did whatever we could to avoid earning the unthinkable label of "having bad manners." People with bad manners were frowned upon, and no one wanted that (or at least no one respectable).

As a young teenager, I was caught "twixt and between" when it came to manners. In a nutshell, I hated them. The young rebel that I was looked upon manners as nothing short of fascism, which at the time I believed meant "being told what to do." I hated being told what to do. But I usually did as I was told anyway because, back then, you could have your "hide tanned" and no one would have even blinked an eye.

I now know that the very manners I once hated were truly an important part of my childhood training. Those little formalities expected of children and enforced by adults, although huddled under the umbrella of being a "well bred person," introduced me to being aware of and caring about other people's feelings. They were the beginnings of the societal training I refer to in Fundamental Three as "genuine interest in and attention to Others."

I had originally thought of naming Fundamental Three "It's all about me," but that would have been a gross oversimplification of the underlying principle. There are two primary entities in our lives: *Self* and *Others*. *Self* is "me, myself and I." *Others* technically includes everyone and everything in our surrounding environment that is a not a part of our body and includes the natural environment surrounding us—the trees, the grass, the dogs and cats, the fences, the sky, the wind—and the people around us every day—friends, acquaintances, waitresses, cashiers, co-workers, people in vehicles next to us, and people walking around us at the mall, to name a few.

But what does "genuine interest in and attention to Others" mean? It means more than just SEEING the environment around us. If we have our eyesight intact, we can all do that most of the time with little effort. Looking more deeply, it means having a genuine consciousness, a seeing, an awareness of, **and** an engagement with, our environment.

We have all been around people who are oblivious to their environment. They stand right in the middle of a walkway blocking the path of a line of people. They don't move when the light turns green. Or they cut in front of us in traffic. They speak loudly on their cell phones in public, and defiantly break in front of ten people patiently waiting in a grocery line. These are the people who have, as we say in the South, bad manners. I will come back to manners in a moment.

All of these examples describe a fundamental blindness to Others that appropriately exists for every child in the early stages of their development. The frightening thing is that this same blindness also exists, in my experience, in MOST adults throughout their lives. Sadly, most adults are not very aware of Others. If they were, they wouldn't be so unkind to their surrounding environment and the people in it.

In the South, when we talk about people who do unkind acts to other people, we use the word *inconsiderate*. "Bob was so inconsiderate of his girlfriend when he didn't comment on her brand new outfit." Men, as you may already know, are notoriously inconsiderate when it comes to noticing women's apparel, hair, make-up, or accessories.

But, let's take a closer look at the word "inconsiderate" as used in this example. It means basically "did not take into consideration" or "did not consider or notice" her in some way. Bob was neither conscious of her outfit, nor her potential desire to have him say something complementary about it. Bob was not, at the time, considerate of Others, which in this case included his girlfriend, her outfit and her feelings.

The reason I am offering this detailed explanation is because we often believe people do not care about us when they act inconsiderately toward us. In many cases, their behavior may not indicate a lack of caring at all. It may simply represent a lack of consciousness. These unconscious oversights are often not acts of malevolence, but are truly simple acts of blindness.

> "...Writers go through this all the time in the beginning. You know, everyone always saying with such enthusiasm, 'Oh I want to read your book. Please, can I read it?' And in the beginning you fall for it because you are just desperate for feedback—at least in the beginning. And then you give it to them and...nothing. You don't hear a word from them. Weeks, months go by. It goes from being the most important thing in their lives in that moment to not a word. At first I would think they didn't like the book...then later realized they just never bothered to read it..."
>
> *Excerpt from coaching session*

When we realize that many people do not make the developmental leap toward awareness of others, we can stop taking these acts of blindness as personal snubs or slights. We can start understanding why OPs do these behaviors, or more specifically in this case, why they don't do them. These explanations do not justify these inconsiderate acts, of course; they simply remove the motive of maliciousness and allow us to interpret them more deeply. Being aware of Fundamental Three may not take away **all** of the pain inherent in an inconsiderate act, but it may help us to avoid reacting defensively with harsh words or equally inconsiderate acts toward the OP.

But what about people who do act maliciously and directly attempt to impose their wishes on other people with little or no care for the feelings they may hurt? These people are another whole breed, known as narcissists, who characteristically are not aware of Others and thus, do not feel connected to, relate to or care for their feelings. Clinically diagnosed narcissists have no capacity to care about another's feelings. They see the world as revolving solely around them and their wishes and desires. Their inability to care for others is reflective of a specific, and often severe, lack of emotional development.

Now, while we all express varying amounts of narcissistic behavior from time to time, for most of us "narcissistic" does not describe the majority of our behavior. Extreme narcissists are a tiny minority in our society. The so-called narcissistic behavior of most people is simply reflective of emotional immaturity. With some training, these people can develop a deeper awareness of Others.

Now, let's get back to manners. As I expressed earlier, as an adult I now have an appreciation for manners that I never had as a child. I understand that in the South, and in other behaviorally bonded communities throughout the U.S., wise adults attempted through the teaching of manners to develop children's awareness of Others, which basically means teaching them that someone else exists besides "you." These Others have feelings and needs that should be considered as we become more perceptually and emotionally mature. As we develop, getting what "I" want is no longer the only matter of importance. The provider of that which I want and their feelings become equally important in the transaction. Every act of manners involves a code of consideration for another person. It moves us from a "me" orientation to a "we" perspective, and the quality of the relationship to each other becomes equally significant.

Fundamental Three does not just apply to intimate relationships. It also applies in business settings. How many of us get frustrated when annual review time comes around? We are given a date on which our review is supposed to take place. We wait and wait for our supervisor to sit down with us for the nervously anticipated conversation. Time passes. We rehearse the possible scenarios in our head.

Mentally, we spend our hoped for pay raise. We make lists of our achievements. Our palms sweat every time our boss asks to see us. Weeks come - - - and go. Maybe my own personal experience was unusually bad, but I remember having to go to my supervisor every year to ask them - no, to beg them - to do my yearly review. And what about projects and special assignments you have slaved over on your "own clock" to complete in record time? How often have your heroic efforts been over looked or unacknowledged? Wouldn't you love to have some authority figure standing over your boss in these situations, tapping their palm with an old fashioned switch while saying, "Now sayyyy thank yooooooou?" I would have.

How many of us working on the floor of a manufacturing plant would have liked to have been spoken to when upper management toured the facilities? How many assistants would like to be asked how their weekends were before being given a list of tasks to do first thing on Monday morning? How many of our working days would have been "made" by a superior who stopped by to give some credit where credit is due? All of these simple actions can produce geometrically significant results. But, they didn't happen because the person who could have made the difference was behaving under the influence of Fundamental Three mentality.

One of the most common (but surprising) questions I have been asked by managers during coaching sessions is, "How do I make employees feel acknowledged? How do I let them know I care?" I consider these questions to be smart and forward thinking because they are asked by managers who realize they want to develop their own skills of acknowledgement. They see the benefit of increasing their ability to maintain a consciousness of and consideration toward Others. My answer to these questions has always been simple. These skills come naturally if you will take a sincere interest in your employees and spend some time just talking with them. To many "old school" managers, this suggestion is looked upon as frightening (see Fundamental One). They would never think of "wasting" all that time just interacting and connecting with employees. But, in today's environment where people have choices and voices, spending a little "just chillin'" time with employees can bear lots of very ripe fruit.

So why is this general lack of awareness of Others so pervasive? Why is it so hard to maintain an awareness of the environment and people around us? Why is it so difficult for many people to engage with those around them? I believe that until we feel that a majority of our personal needs are met, we cannot begin to acknowledge, let alone give, to others around us. Until I get some sense of fulfillment within myself, I have nothing to give YOU—including money, love, attention, sex, and verbal encouragement. Anything that is presently mine that I **could** give to you, I cannot give away until I have reached a point where I am emotionally "full." Until I feel fulfilled, you will get little or nothing significant from me.

Unfortunately, so few of us feel fulfilled. In reality, we have little to give our loved ones, let alone other people around us in various settings once we leave our homes. We are so busy trying to "get ours" that we are easily annoyed by any requests asked of us by others. In the all too common state of "I ain't got enough for me," we are only interested in Self. What "I" need and want cripples my ability to meaningfully engage with Others.

This portrait may seem overly pessimistic. Of course many people in the world have done and are doing conscious, meaningful and caring things for Others. But in the long term, ultimately we can only give to the same level we feel fulfilled in our lives.

There is some reason for hope. Recently, our experience of being a part of a "world culture" (think of it as a huge Other) is expanding in the face of natural disasters such as Hurricane Katrina in the U.S., the typhoon in Indonesia that killed over 100,000, or the devastating earthquake in China. There are Others out there. These disasters woke us, for a moment at least, from our self-centeredness. In the blink of an eye, our nation's hearts went out to Others. We bonded as a nation with some Others outside ourselves. We experienced the same national awareness after the devastation of September 11.

The fact we did so tells us that while awareness of Others is a rare commodity in general, anyone can raise their own awareness anytime they wish. With a little interest and attention to our unawareness of

Others, we can begin to change our scope of consciousness immediately. Maybe we should take a lesson from my own Southern roots before it disappears in the wake of cell phones, computer e-mail, and every other technological means of avoiding human contact.

"...So I'm sitting there stuck next to this seventy-year old geezer who is talking to me and I 'm trying to be polite and all while he's talking, feigning at least some interest, and he says, 'You know I used to use a state of the art reel to reel tape stereo system for parties. It fills an entire room in the basement, and I used to play music at all the USO parties for the World War II veterans.' And for some stupid reason I say, 'Can I see it?' I'm not believing that it came out of my mouth.

All of a sudden I see his face light up and his voice gets all animated...it was like I stuck a firecracker up his butt. I didn't even want to see the stuff really, I don't know why I asked him in the first place, but man...he jumped up out of his chair and started running around all excited and now I'm getting all excited to see this stuff. He takes me to his 'sound room' and showed me everything he had. EVERYTHING. And it really was fun just watching him get so excited that I asked about his tape system.

I made his day...no his year just asking about it. I felt kinda bad later because I really didn't care at first about anything he had to say."

Excerpt from actual coaching session

What would happen if you actually took a moment to smile at someone behind a counter instead of ignoring them while talking to someone else on your cell phone? Would a "please" during a request or a "thank you" after it is filled be too painful to say? Watch other people's positive reactions to these and other simple acts of appreciation and gratitude. You might be pleasantly surprised. Besides, it is just good manners.

So once we become aware of Others, as this Fundamental suggests, we might notice that we are hesitant to become involved with them or to interact with them, even in some small way. When was the last time you had a friendly chat with a total stranger? It has probably been a while. And why is it so hard to be polite to Others these days? Why didn't you acknowledge the waiter or person behind the coffee counter today with some smile or act of kindness? Are you afraid (see Fundamental One) that it would make you appear weak? Why is it we always are trying to look so "cool" and detached, instead of friendly and kind?

These questions bring us to another doorway that can be cracked open a bit by Fundamental Four.

Most relationships, and their recurring problems, are based on power dynamics.

> Behaviors you might see from OPs include: refusal to apologize when clearly wrong; consciously withholding approval from people; acts of blaming others while taking no responsibility for their own actions, betrayal of previous relational agreements; erratic, sometimes aggressive behaviors; or emotionality uncharacteristic of the OPs personality in the past.

I have participated in, counseled people in and witnessed many different relationships throughout my years. Since professionally I am often exposed at deep levels to many relationships that are going through challenges, I decided that before I could become comfortable with the idea of getting married, I wanted to find a model of a relationship or marriage that I admired personally—a relationship that exhibited true caring and genuine loving. In my quest to find such an inspirational relationship, I "researched" relationships in a number of different settings. Basically, this means I shut up and listened when I went to events.

Parties were always one of the most productive research venues. I always watched how couples interacted with each other while in the public "social eye." I was appalled for most of my thirties as I witnessed "loving" couple after "loving" couple begin to beat each other up (verbally, of course) shortly after arriving at a party or event, once the social niceties were over. Snide comments here and sarcastic comments there were punctuated with rolling eyes of frustration, delivered with exaggerated gusto for the benefit of on-looking friends.

After a short mingling period, husbands and wives often separated to their respective gender corners where verbal barbs and complaints about partners were followed by laughs and nodding heads. Current events discussions focused on how he/she did this or that and was such a "pain in the a___". I witnessed this scenario so often that I truly was concerned about whether anyone was happy after several years of marriage.

The image of venting my frustration with life and my partner through constant bickering and barb throwing was not my idea of a pleasant life. Yet the majority of what I was seeing fell into those kinds of behaviors. I watched so many couples engage in this verbal abuse ritual that I came to the conclusion, after a period of time, that the institution of marriage must not be conducive to loving relationships. For many years I believed Woody Allen's banner statement that "marriage was the death of all hope."

"I never want to get married."

(Friends): "You will, you will, you just haven't found the right person."

"No really, I'm thirty-five years old and I've been in several long term monogamous relationships and loved them all, but I don't want to get married. There is no single cell in me that can make the leap from loving a monogamous relationship, to spending my life—-living with someone for the rest of my life."

(Friends): Oh come on...you just haven't found the right one."

"No seriously, and I'll tell you why...present company excluded of course..." (Friends laugh)

"...I've never met or seen a couple where I've ever said, 'Wow, that's what I want!' Except one, and they have been together for thirty-five years and they have an open marriage. I'm not saying that's what I'm looking for, the open part, I'm just saying they are the only couple that I've ever witnessed over time that truly are excited being with each other. You can see it in how they are when they are together and how they talk to each other.

I don't even know if it's the open marriage that contributes to their happiness because I am sure there are plenty of open marriages that have failed, but every other couple I see seems so bitter. The husband can't take the first sip of beer standing around us all, just the guys, before he says, 'Thank God—no wives out here.' And then he starts bitching about his wife while the other husbands roar with laughter and tell stories of their own. And then, and invariably this happens…like some kind of primal animal marking ritual, they all turn to ME and ask if I'm married. Like maybe I was the only one NOT laughing hard enough. Truthfully, I probably looked horrified.

"'No,' I tell them and they all laugh again as if it's some married guy cue or something."

"'Lucky man!' they say. 'Lucky man!' And I'm telling you, except for that one couple, I've never seen a couple that is still happy after five years, let alone thirty-five."

"Then I go to the kitchen for another beer and what do I hear? The wives are telling snide jokes about how lazy, bored, dull, or quiet their husbands are. They are topping each other to see who has the dullest husband. 'If Jack says three sentences to me before he gets to his television sports games, I consider it our sex for the night,' one says. 'And that's all he's getting too!' she says to squeals of laughter from the other wives.

Let me tell ya, if marriage is a product that someone is selling, they need a new marketing campaign 'cuz its nothing I want to be a part of."

From actual conversation

Even though I was very disturbed about the bitterness I saw between couples, I was still curious enough to question it. I was amazed at the number of seemingly unhappy marriages I witnessed, and I was determined to find out where the genuinely affectionate marriages were hiding. I had concluded they must exist somewhere—or the divorce rate would certainly rise above its traditional 50% rate.

I originally theorized that the trouble with relationships in general, especially long-term relationships like marriage was caused by poor communication skills of the partners. I believed that if the partners had better skills with which to communicate with each other, maybe they would be more able to work out their underlying resentments and anger. I believed this theory until I spent a few more years watching my counseling clients hash out their differences in my office—together and individually. What I was witnessing in counseling sessions was actually a process radically different than I originally expected. Yes, people did need better skills to communicate with each other. But their lack of technical skills was not causing the underlying resentments that soured their interactions with their partners. Even after the process of working through their issues, the resentment and anger was still hanging over their future interactions. If the resentments were truly caused by the lack of communication skills, then the anger should dissipate rapidly between the partners once clarity in communication was attained. As far as I could tell, the resentments were not dissipating to any great degree.

It was then I theorized that the majority of the relational problems I witnessed were **not** caused by a lack of healthy communication techniques at all. Instead, they seemed to be caused by pre-established, ongoing, power dynamics within the relationship, particularly the power game I call "passing the guilt bat."

"Passing the guilt bat" is something I first witnessed with a couple I knew personally. They had married in their twenties and already had two children as they began their thirties. He was a wealthy businessman; she stayed home to take care of the children. On one particular eye-opening day, I was visiting with the husband, Jack (not his real name). We were sitting on the porch discussing the day and sipping beer. His wife, Diane (not her real name), was across the street browsing through a wide variety of miscellaneous "someone else's treasures" at a neighbor's yard sale. After a few minutes of conversation, Jack and I were distracted as Diane came scurrying back across the street to where we were sitting, a pile of wrinkled clothes thrown over one shoulder. With a victorious smile, she approached us. "I got some great stuff cheap and some new outfits that were never worn but once," she said, smiling excitedly.

Without a moment's pause, Jack exploded. "Why did you spend our money?" And, louder still, "Who said you could do that?" His anger hung in the air, as he lowered his voice and challenged his stunned wife. "Don't you dare bring that stuff up here!"

Diane was obviously shocked at his anger. I was stunned and appalled.

Jack continued his warning. "You take them back…now…take them back…don't come up here with those clothes."

Diane stopped dead, mouth open.

I tried to release some tension by jumping into the middle of the thickness. "God, Jack, what is wrong with you?"

As my nervously delivered comment fell on deaf ears, the yard sale hostess walked up, and came to a slow stop next to Diane. Realizing he was now being observed by the yard sale hostess and me, Jack mumbled something unintelligible and stormed off into the house. After a heavy moment, and with a sigh, Diane walked past me uncomfortably, following behind the steps of her husband. The yard sale hostess shrugged, turned and walked back across the street. After a few slow sips of beer, and a few moments spent scratching my head, I went inside to join my friends. Nothing else was said about the incident, by them or by me, while I was there.

I assumed that the incident must have been related to some "hot button" money issue they had fought about earlier, but found out later this was not the case. If the reason behind the outburst was not an on-going money issue or a specific rule around spending that had been broken, then why had they had this fight?

Over time, I witnessed this couple engage in several similar outbursts. They involved different situations. She berated him at times and he berated her at times. While the topics of the fights changed (money, sex, duties not completed, time issues, to name a few) a thematic pattern seemed to form. No matter what the topic was, one person would stand for the "right" and "virtuous" side and verbally beat down the person on the "wrong" and "selfish" side. Their arguments followed a pattern of "I'm right, you're wrong, now give me the bat and take your beating!" Broken down into this basic structure, I realized I was witnessing a power dynamic.

Generally, a power dynamic involves two people engaging in a play for power by attempting to get "one up" on, or to have the upper hand over, their partner. In this game, whoever effectively throws the most guilt on the other party wins that round and temporarily maintains the upper hand, and, thus, the power.

I learned later that this particular couple's power dynamic was established early in their relationship. While money was not truly a problem for them, it was the major area in which they "passed the bat." Jack was the breadwinner and controlled the money tightly (power role #1). Diane felt controlled whenever she spent money, even though they could afford it. She took **her** righteous indignation out on him whenever he talked about buying a high priced item he wanted (power role #2). So they passed the bat (angry criticisms) back and forth, delivering strong whacks to each other in the process (power dynamics).

Often their financial arguments would circle around several subjects until they came to rest on the central, irrefutably important and righteous theme of "protecting the financial future of the children." When a high ideal whose appropriateness cannot be questioned is interjected into a seemingly unrelated argument, I call this move the "rush to the moral high ground." In the throes of a heated argument, angry partners will choose whatever high ground is available that will make their objections and anger look motivated by high morals and virtue and not just sheer rage or revenge for the last whacking they themselves received. The underlying dynamics might look like this:

Partner one says: "I'm not yelling at you for buying (the object in question) because you did the same to me yesterday…. I am yelling at you to protect our CHILDREN and their financial well being." With this statement, partner one has taken the moral high ground.

The energy expressed behind the words is clear—she/he is obviously only interested in the children's well being, so TAKE THAT! The bottom-line justification of this dynamic is simply, "I am GOOD, you are BAD, hand me the bat." Within a power dynamic, partners are continually on watch to take advantage of moments when they can rush to the moral high ground, claim the bat, and "hit" their partners rather than being "hit" themselves.

One of the surest signs that a power dynamic exists within a relationship is behavior that shows that one partner is enjoying any pain experienced by the other. Whether it is magnifying a partner's embarrassment in front of others, laughing cruelly at a mistake they made, or an exaggerated "Aha!" when a friend agrees with them and not their partner, these behaviors show the need to score a "one up" on their partner. If the "one up" is scored in public, all the better.

Power dynamics can start as innocent competition between couples. Couples often play little one-up games such as who knows more about certain subjects than the other, or who knows who better, or who won the last board or card game they played. All of these things without an underlying resentment can present themselves as playful ribbing between partners. But if playful ribbing comes too close to an underlying resentment and a power dynamic can easily hatch and become something bigger. If one partner feels publicly embarrassed by a comment or action by the other partner, the offended partner may retaliate by looking for a chance to throw back a "gotcha" statement in front of friends. Back and forth the volley goes until verbally *bantering*, a playful activity that may have actually been harmless in the beginning stages of the relationship, becomes verbal *battering*.

Once a power dynamic is started, it is not only hard to stop, but it also spreads to many different areas in the relationship. One day you may stand on the high ground and yell at me for always being late. The next day I may "get" you for not letting the dog out soon enough. I may throw you a line like: "Don't you care about anyone else but yourself?"

Sex is another notorious battleground for power dynamics between partners (as you may already know). "You got me good last night in front of my friends about spending money. Now see if you are going to get any sex TONIGHT!" I honestly believe that the REAL reason for the stereotypical lack of sex after marriage is because it is the most common arena in which power dynamics are acted out. How many times have you heard on T.V. or in a movie a line that in essence says, "If you do that, forget about sleeping with me anytime soon."

People learn quickly that sex (or the lack of it) is a nuclear weapon in power dynamics. You embarrass me... you get no sex. Often the lack of sex between married partners is really not even about withholding sex as much as it is a symptom of emotional disenchantment. How can I feel sexual toward someone who constantly humiliates me or criticizes me? As the emotional disenchantment between partners grows, the power games increase and the sediment layers of unexpressed rage pile up. Goodbye sexual feelings.

In families with children, power dynamics get even trickier. When children are used as the home plate on which you stand as you wield the guilt bat, it is harder to figure out if parental duties are being assigned to punish the other partner or if they legitimately need to be done.

In marriages with babies and younger children, time becomes another interesting venue where the power dynamics game is played out. The stay at home parent (if there is one) complains: "I've had the children all day (moral high ground), now you take them and let ME go out for a while (you uncaring jerk)." This battle cry is thrown back and forth between the parents as they stampede up and down the moral high ground of "time with the children." The more time one parent spends with the children, the bigger the bat they get to use on the other parent. As the children grow up, the bat can take the form of, "You're not spending enough time with YOUR children." Whenever the phrase "your daughter" or "your son" is used in a sentence (usually with an angry tone), you know a power dynamic is being played out.

Sex, time, money, and duties are all ripe areas in which relationship power dynamics take root. While these areas are commonly conflictual in relationships at some time or another, two characteristics usually differentiate a normal conflict (that is capable of being worked through) and a power dynamic. The first characteristic is a need to be "right or justified" (the moral high ground position). The second is a "Gotcha!" quality. A wife could say to a husband, "I need a break... badly!" after the husband gets home from work without either: 1) becoming the martyr to prove how righteous and caring she has been all day (and thus justified in requesting a break), or 2) using the request like a bat to gleefully punish the other partner (Gothcha!).

Sometimes I have heard a partner involved in this kind of dynamic say, "Look, I know you need a break, but you don't have to blast me to get it." To me, this kind of comment is a good sign because it shows openness to communicating about the situation. If the frustrated, stay at home parent responds, his/her response can be a telltale indication of the power dynamics that exist between the parents. Apologies are rare within power dynamics, so I listen for them to differentiate between a true power struggle and a momentary conflict where one partner just hit their limit and blew up. If the frustrated stay at home parent says something similar to "I'm sorry, honey, I was just pulling my hair out by the time you came in," it appears that the normal stress of child rearing won out for the moment but that the guilt bat is safely tucked away in the dugout.

To see if we can get a clearer picture of this dynamic, let's look at this same situation with a little bit of a different twist. Let's say, that instead of apologizing, the stay at home parent says, "Well, if you really cared about me and the kids, I wouldn't even have to ask!" This is a definite indication that the fed-up spouse is wielding the guilt bat and that a power struggle is in full swing.

So why are so many relationships based on power dynamics? The reason is rooted in issues of boundaries and self esteem. Because so few people have a healthy self-esteem, they do not feel justified in setting appropriate boundaries for themselves. Because they feel unworthy at some deep level, they cannot emotionally justify setting a boundary or making a legitimate request. To feel "OK" about making the request, they have to use a moral high ground play to justify it. In other words, when I do not feel justified or worthy enough to ask you to take the children for a while, I have to prove that you OWE it to me because of my selfless and virtuous behavior. When I do not feel worthy or justified in saying, "No" (setting a boundary), to one of your previous requests, I have to devise a payback request to get you back. This dynamic can go on and on throughout a relationship. If a partner is hit too many times with the other partner's righteous indignation, the layers of resentment may get too deep to be easily shoveled out into the open and dissipated. At this point, reducing the resentment between partners begins to feel hopeless and many couples simply give up.

Wherever there is a lack of courageous and clear communication in relationship, power dynamics breed. Unfortunately, because courageous communication between partners is so rare in our society, power dynamics flourish. It is not that people don't have the SKILLS to communicate. Many people do exhibit these skills in less intimate settings, such as work or community activities. But in intimate relationships, where the emotional stakes are higher, partners often lack the COURAGE to communicate openly and honestly with their mates. "Why don't you just tell them what you need?" is one of the most common questions I ask in my practice. "Oh, I couldn't tell them THAT," is my clients' most common answer.

It is interesting to me that couples are more comfortable avoiding honest communication (and letting resentment grow) than having a brief uncomfortable discussion that could clear everything up instantly. Rather than express their anger and resentment honestly, they express it through sarcasm or ridicule. Rather than vent their resentment directly, they look for ways to get back at their partner indirectly through power dynamics.

In corporate settings, power dynamics are usually much more subtle. A guilt bat is too crude a weapon in this arena. In corporate power dynamics, the ice pick is the back stabbing weapon of choice. Innocent looking enough, an ice pick rarely kills with the first stab.

It is most effective for the slow mortal wounding used in political power games. No guilt bat is needed because everyone playing the political power game believes they inherently deserve everything for which they are fighting. Since they believe they are already "deserving," they usually don't feel the need to justify their power plays through inflicting guilt or standing on moral high ground. They simply grab what they want however they can. I may back stab behind the scenes and take your position or power, but I deserved it anyway, so no justification is needed. In fact, I may be openly rewarded for it.

Moral high ground (and thus the guilt bat) may sometimes be used within peer employee relations, because in this arena, we are equals in the hierarchy and the conflicted participants do not have enough job title power to control each other. Since we cannot use the power of higher position to get what we want, we will often use our own Stress and Time as guilt bats on others.

For example, I used to be the director of an alcohol and drug rehabilitation unit in a hospital. As a manager and a supervisor, I attended a number of weekly meetings with all levels of management. A personal goal of mine was to never be late to a meeting of any kind, no matter what it took to leave the situation I was previously engaged in. One director from another unit took another approach. She would walk in late to every upper management meeting to prove how overwhelmingly stressful her workload was and how difficult it was for her to leave her unit. "Please don't be mad at me for being late. I was so busy trying to solve a huge conflict up on my unit, I lost track of time," she would say as she sat down and put her face in her hands, exasperated from the recent stress she had endured. "You can't be mad at me because look how stressed I am," was her unspoken message. I was amazed by how well this behavior seemed to work on some of the upper managers, who were supposedly well versed in psychologically motivated tactics. Others rightfully saw this behavior as a ploy for power. We had not only held up the meeting for her, but she was also able to play up the enormous stress of her job. This is an example of an attempt to make one's self seem more important and powerful by making people wait. It is a passive-aggressive method used by people to artificially elevate their power over people.

Another popular workplace power dynamic is "whoever stays the longest at work wins." In many conversations with a former boss, I would exhale as I listened to him talk about never leaving the office before 7 P.M., thus proving his strong work ethic and commitment to the job. Of course, he failed to mention that his daily "work" schedule included an hour-long mid-day jog and a two-hour dinner before leaving. By putting in the "longest hours of anyone" each day, he painted the picture of working harder than everyone, therefore justifying his salary and position (for which, in my observation, he actually felt unworthy). My experience has been that the more efficient and autonomous a staff is allowed to become, the less crisis appears within the team, and the more relaxed the team's manager appears. Unfortunately, too often in the business setting whoever **appears** to have the most stress and the least available time is viewed as working harder, whether they are truly contributing or not.

Well, we have come to the end of this chapter but there is a problem with ending our discussion of Fundamental Four now. There are so many examples of various power dynamics that there is no possible way to address them all. Some of the tactics used in power struggles are so subtle that you are not sure if you are being hit with a knife or an ice pick. Either way, being on the receiving end of a power struggle dynamic hurts like hell, even if you don't know what the weapon looks like.

Power is such a primary driving force behind people's behaviors; it pervades all walks of life and all areas of social interaction. Remember, Power is most often grabbed for, used, and abused by people as a defense for their fears. Fearful people will use power plays in an attempt to "scare off" people that they perceive as being more powerful than they are. Their actions state, "I am powerful!" Yet under that expressed bravado, emotionally they are whispering, "I am scared" (see Fundamental One).

So what do these people hope to gain by accumulating all this power? What is their goal? That, not surprisingly, brings us to the next Fundamental.

Everyone is rushing toward the white picket fence.

Behaviors you might see from OPs include: relationships progressing to engagement/marriage at an extremely fast rate; relationships progressing to marriage in spite of repeated destructive or hurtful behaviors by one or both of the partners; inability to acknowledge the negative/destructive behaviors of partners, friends, etc., even when apparent to others; difficulty leaving hurtful relationships/partners/situations.

"I was on a date last weekend. Do you have this problem with your dates? They are interviewing me for marriage from moment one. The second we hit the car, what looks like casual conversation is actually an 'are you marriage material' interview. I'm serious. It goes from 'what do you do for a living' to 'do you want to have children'. She said this to me I swear five minutes in—-third or fourth question! I laughed at it thinking that she was joking or doing some stereotype joke. Nope, she was not joking. 'Are you serious,' I said. 'We haven't even had dinner and you're asking if I want kids?' She looks at me with this 'I am dead serious' stare like some cyborg interrogator. 'I just need to know if I am wasting my time here,' she says. I say, 'wasting your time...we haven't even made it to the restaurant yet.'"

From actual conversation

In Fundamentals One through Four, we have talked about the power of Fear and how it influences our behaviors and decisions. Assuming everyone is terrified (see Fundamental One), the primary motivation underlying many of our actions is our desire to reduce the Fear in our lives. This fundamental drive—to reduce Fear—is also the primary motivation behind Fundamental Five. One way to reduce Fear is to insulate ourselves in some kind of psychological or physical "structure" that feels "safe." In the United States, one of our favorite symbols of safety and security is the notion of the "white picket fence." The "white picket fence" is the archetypal symbol of home, happiness, family, financial stability and emotional security.

A close look at the "white picket fence" ideal reveals that there are generally three components to the picture intended to help answer three basic questions:

How will I make money?

Will I get married?

Will I have children?

It is fascinating to realize that what are arguably our three most important life decisions are usually the least thought out. Most people answer these questions—or have them answered for them—very early in their lives without thinking them through to any depth. A whole lifetime can be structured by the answers, which are often made on autopilot!

For many people, living out the answers to these questions establishes their claim to the white picket fence, thus creating some sense of safety and insulating them from that big, dangerous world out there. I think of these three goals as a safety trifecta: all you have to do is get a job, a spouse and kids—and everything else will fall into place.

The first question (career/job/making money) is usually primary, "and unavoidable, because most of us need money to live: and in our society, money, job and career go hand-in-hand. Most of us do not have a large range of answers from which to choose when it comes to financial safety. Unless we are financially favored and have been born into or married wealth, most of us will spend a good portion of our adult lives working. The question becomes not if we will work, but what we will do for work.

Let's look at the second component of our "white picket fence" trifecta.

In my observation, most people do not spend any significant amount of time pondering whether or not they will marry. In our culture, it is still a primary, collective belief that "being married" is normal, and that "choosing to be single" is a deviation from the norm. Even the age at which we marry is factored into our "normal" rating. Too young is frowned on because it is unsafe. Yet for many people, marrying too late (however that is defined) is seen as a sign of immaturity or unsuitability. When interviewing candidates for a position, many large, established companies see being married as a sign of stability and maturity. Even family and friends will jokingly ask, "What is wrong with you?" if you haven't married by what is perceived to be an "appropriate" age.

An overwhelming majority of today's adults still discuss marriage as a "when", not an "if," event. In fact, to shorten the debate should the topic come up, many singles answer the marriage question with a brief "eventually" or "soon", rather than "I am thinking about that one."

Sometimes people find a creative way around the first question (career/making money) by jumping to the second question (marriage) and marrying someone with the means to support them, thus "gaining possession" of two (and maybe even three) legs of the safety stool at one time. However, marriage itself, whether or not accompanied by wealth, is so symbolic of safety that many people marry partners who are clearly unable to support themselves, let alone anyone else. The rationale here: "Love is all we need."

Here's my point: Because people are so naturally in need of safety to stave off Fear, and marriage is seen as one-third of the safety trifecta (true or not), people often rush to accomplish it. This rushing is usually counterproductive because a successful relationship that will lead to a successful marriage inherently needs more time to develop than most people will allow.

Often clients and friends have told me that once they get married, once they find that perfect someone, everything will be "all right." I have witnessed person after person marry either too young or too soon after meeting a partner because they don't want to be alone or date anymore. I have seen people marry to get away from parents, dysfunctional homes, careers, or other unpleasant life circumstances. Some people marry out of boredom or to just do something "crazy." Britney Spears' famous thirty-six hour marriage was said to fall into this category. Once married, most people seem to believe they are "almost home," so to speak.

Sadly this is not necessarily true. I believe that most people have such a strong, unconscious need to feel safe that they marry the wrong people for the wrong reasons. They marry people they know too little about in too short of a time, and this is a major reason that the U.S. divorce rate hovers around 50%. The institution of marriage is not the problem. WHY people are marrying is the problem. If I am marrying to reduce Fear (see Fundamental One), that motivation compresses the amount of time I am willing to spend to reasonably—and realistically—get to know and evaluate a partner. In fact, in our society, we are encouraged to believe that Love is not supposed to be rational. Instead, we are taught that, ideally, Love is a matter of the heart and based on a deep emotional connection to our love partner. Unfortunately, people motivated by Fear will usually not allow themselves the luxury of approaching relationship with an open heart, or a discerning mind.

The third leg of the safety trifecta, children, is another little thought out portion of the "white picket fence" safety scenario. What could be safer or more secure than the image of children playing inside the fence? Nothing completes the picture better than 2.3 "mini-me's" running around a manicured yard. In today's society, rare is the person who doesn't want children after marriage! Like those people who remain unmarried in their thirties, married couples who do not have children are often looked upon by the masses with:

Pity ("They must be unable to have them."); or

Scorn ("They are just too selfish.")

Why should people care if others have children or not? Because they love their own version of the white picket fence, and they expect others to want the same version for themselves.

I believe, at its core, moving toward the white picket fence is a worthy goal for most people. It is the rushing sense of impatience—"I have to get there to survive"—that creates issues later in life. Because we are making huge decisions based on Fear (see Fundamental One, yet again), we often 'wake up' years later feeling dissatisfied.

Fundamental Five, I believe, is the key reason for mid-life crises. One day, our awareness changes and we feel our lives have become overly sterilized and boring. We often wake up at mid-life and realize that many of our life decisions were never decided by us at all; they were decided by our Fears. Through this lens it appears that we are not looking at our life at all, but someone else's. In fact, this is true.

Most of us spend the first half of our lives living someone else's life—the life we were told to live—the life we *thought* we wanted because parents, tradition, the culture, religion, or other influencing 'powers that be' TOLD us to live that life, TOLD us this was the life we wanted. We lived this life for years thinking it was our own idea. But a light goes on one day and we realize it was not. We wake up one day and think, "This isn't what I want to do, how I want to live—I don't even enjoy it!"

It is usually only in the second half of life that people have a chance to live a life of their own design. Sadly, only a relatively small percentage of people will take advantage of this opportunity. Asking the question, "Is this the life I want to lead?" is enormously threatening and risky. More often than not, it will not even be asked. Other types of Fear take over at this point: the Fear of rocking the boat and the Fear of the unknown. Rather than risk change, the treadmill will continue moving and most people will simply continue walking it without question. They inevitably take their places in the procession of the living dead and turn themselves into passionless robots. These people work very hard to keep the boat of life steady and to avoid enacting a mid-life crisis.

It is easy to see why. We are all too familiar with the stereotypical description of the mid-life crisis: an older man (a gender stereotype because women also have these crises) comes home with the red sports car, begins dating a younger woman, or has an affair. I believe that many affairs occur because the partners married initially for safety and, in fact, they achieve it in marriage. Yet this sought after safety can become a double-edged sword. After several years of experiencing safety within a marriage, a person relaxes. This relaxation opens a door to previously unknown or unacknowledged emotional needs, new life ambitions, or even new physical desires. The comfort of years of safety inside a secure marriage may bring forth a new level of courage and an internal restlessness that has never before been experienced.

In short, when we feel safe, we begin to change. Feelings, moods, desires, wishes and dreams—everything begins to change. In an attempt to quench these newly felt emotions and dreams, people will often pursue some form of unusual, risky or exotic hobby or experience. The need for stimulation can take the form of new or unusual interests, changes in the types of friends the searching partner wants, or in life, travel or career change.

Here is the irony of relationships: While most of us get into them to live happily ever after, that is, for stability, the truth is that if everything in the relationship goes exactly RIGHT, people inside the relationship CHANGE, causing instability. Weird, huh? One or both partners inside a relationship that goes WELL will change because of the influence of that loving container. Due to the healing nature of the best relationships/marriages I have seen, previously shy men (and, yes, some of them were **painfully** shy) suddenly find the courage to talk to attractive women at parties. I have seen sexually repressed women come into their full, confident sexuality because of a supportive relationship. The marriage, in these cases, acts as an emotional cauldron of safety that brings forth new strengths and characteristics in the partners. Unfortunately for this whole positive process, both partners usually do not change at the same time or in the same psychological areas.

If a partner who is not experiencing change at the moment (let's call them the "status quo" partner) is supportive of the process of the changing partner and does not become threatened, the changing partner may pursue their new interests and friends without sending a negative jolt through the relationship. If the status quo partner becomes threatened, or if the changing partner's desires go against their previous relationship agreements, the changing partner will most likely "go underground" and they will find secret ways to pursue these needs. This, of course, opens up a whole new can of very squiggly worms.

In relationships that are not strong enough or flexible enough to allow the changing partner to express his/her newfound courage and interests, that partner may begin to look outward. If one or both partners is threatened, and the Fear of staying stagnant is **greater** than the Fear of change, the changing partner may look for others who appreciate his/her new found powers and interests.

This is often where affairs begin. Affairs, for the most part, are not vehicles of love connection; they are more often a revisiting of the emotional playground that was left quickly behind at a young age when relationship choices were made out of Fear. Rather than spending time and effort improving one's self esteem and dealing with interpersonal awkwardness as younger, dating adults, many people skip this experimental and developmental phase and jump straight to "safety" by marrying young.

The influence of Fundamental Five also applies to relationship situations outside of marriage. An example is the rise of what I call the "I hate dating" epidemic. Now I should say here that many "twenty-somethings" of today have found a way to bypass the whole "I have to call someone to ask for a date" routine. Many "twenty-somethings" these days move in homogenous packs of males and females and plan to meet somewhere to party together. This is a much less vulnerable process because all you have to do is show up to the meeting place without the vulnerability of asking someone if they want to go out with you. This next section is for the people who still take the risk of making a phone call to someone to request a date.

For many singles, the ins and outs and uncertainties of dating lose their charm over time, especially as we get older. It is not that the social portion of dating is truly daunting. It is the recurring vulnerability we feel while dating that takes its toll on us. When we go out on dates, we try to put our best face forward, even as we sit in the middle of all our human frailties, insecurities, and vulnerabilities. We are faced with the best and the worst in ourselves. We are uncomfortable and challenged when we see these weaknesses in others because we are reminded of our own shortcomings. Frailties seem magnified on dates because we are so busy trying to impress each other, and warding off the dreaded demon—rejection. Many modern dating innovations, for example, Internet dating, have sprung from the desire to lessen the likelihood of experiencing rejection. Speed dating, a more recent "I hate dating" invention, simply tries to dramatically shorten the entire horrendous process.

I was thirty-two at the time and I walked into my favorite dance place. This was like '82 or something. Everyone at the place that night was especially fantastic looking. It was a night of beautiful people, even the guys were dressed better than usual. The women, though, were spectacular. It was like a dream come true. A models' party—and the whole room, it seemed, was…it was like that Woody Allen movie…you know with the happy train and the sad train? Woody is on the bleak, ugly train with all the old, horrible, ugly people and he's looking across into the adjoining train car…the HAPPY train with a gorgeous Sharon Stone drinking champagne with all the beautiful people, confetti flying, dancing, laughter. Well that night I am on the Happy train.

I get a drink and to my right as I order are six gorgeous, mini-dressed women, legs to forever, in their late twenties. I can tell it's a bachelorette party. I ask, casually, the girl next to me who is part of the party, "Who is the lady of honor tonight?" or something like that and she turns to me in this "I'm squaring my shoulders and delivering the answer cuz you asked me the magic question" kind of dramatic way. She throws her fist toward my face. My head jerks back a little because she is not throwing it at me hard or anything…but it surprised me…and her fist is like six inches in front of my face.

"I am." She says. "See my ring? See my diamond? You know what this means? It means I no longer have to deal with the likes of you or anyone like you again!" She snapped her hand back and turned around.

"Safety at last." I thought to myself.

From actual conversation

My own experience with dating was mixed, but overall, I would say it was "pleasant." My major challenge was controlling my tendency to be honest and blunt with people. From our discussion of Fundamental One, we know that people are very uncomfortable with blunt openness and honesty. Most dates are ideally supposed to be safe, sterile exercises designed to (hopefully) avoid making anyone too uncomfortable. In order to play fair and stay in the dating game, I tried very hard to be "polite" and to hold my tongue.

Then, while trudging through one particularly "bad date" in my thirties, something enlightening—and enlivening—happened! I was having lunch (you know, a "safe" date) with a woman I met through a friend. While she was very physically attractive, by the time we had ordered appetizers it was very clear to both of us that we just didn't click. I paused for a minute, realizing that we had a good, long forty-five minutes or so ahead of us. Rather than tough it out while being polite, I decided to surrender to my desire to be honest.

I cleared my throat and said, "Look, it is obvious to both of us that we are wired differently. I know we are not each other's type, but we are already here and our food will be coming in a minute… so why don't we make the best of it."

She did not look surprised in the least. In fact, she smiled, albeit somewhat faintly.

"So," I continued, "since we will most likely never see each other again, why don't we find out as much about each other as we can in the time left. Maybe we will learn something about each other that we wouldn't have if we were busying ourselves trying to impress each other?"

She gave me a huge smile of relief, and an enthusiastic "Okay!"

We had a magnificently interesting, personable conversation. We told each other things we never would have if we were trying to keep our "dating armor" intact. I felt safe enough to ask several personal questions that I would usually save for "later dates." Instead of the usual "you don't fit my list of requirements—so see ya" attitude, we worked with the vulnerability and insecurity of the situation and had lunch as two important strangers might—with curiosity and acceptance of differences.

It was actually one of the most wonderfully relaxed lunches I ever had with an important stranger. I like to think of all strangers as important (see Fundamental Three—"Awareness of Others") because they can teach me something if I am vulnerable enough to connect with them. What could have been a dreadful lunch filled with inane small talk, turned into a special sharing between two people, both of whom were looking for a special someone.

After a satisfying and empowering encounter, we said our goodbyes. We have never seen each other again, but that is the least important aspect of our short, but significant, relationship. I often think back on this lunch as a reminder that interactions that might initially seem uncomfortable—or even intolerable—can be turned into something special if both parties allow themselves to be open and vulnerable in the moment.

How many times do we lose the chance to connect with someone because we are too busy checking off our "perfect" guy/gal list and ignoring the person who sits in front of us? Are we too busy rushing toward the white picket fence to notice or interact with someone who does not quickly fit our paper description of "the one?" A hazard of rushing too quickly toward the white picket fence is that we tend to dismissively speed past or run over a lot of people on our way there, leaving a wake of hurt feelings behind us. People who ponder Fundamental Three and integrate awareness of others into their interactions will find fewer crushed or ignored people strewn behind them on their quests for the perfect partner.

Before we leave the topic of "lists", let me clarify my beliefs on that subject. A list can be a useful tool for clarifying what is important for you in a partner, and it can help focus your energy on what you are looking for. Although this technique works well for some people, I have noticed that a number of people fall in love with someone who doesn't fit their list. Many times, this non-list person will show up when the person is dating someone who does fit their list, but who does not make their heart flutter.

"What should I do?" a client will ask.

"Forget the list and listen to your heart!" I say.

While lists may force us to focus our minds on our likes and dislikes and help us to define our priorities, they should only be seen as a mental exercise—not a relationship Bible. Lists should never overrule the heart. I recommend that we think of lists as rough guidelines that change as we mature in life. Can you imagine how different your list at age sixteen would be from your list at age thirty? How will your list differ in ten years? How about thirty years? Hard to tell, isn't it?

Although I feel most people would fare significantly better in the relationship arena if they would just follow their hearts, the need to quiet our Fear, and to reach a safe haven, is often stronger than our desire to love and be loved. An unconscious rush toward the white picket fence often leaves little time for our heart to "feel out" a potential partner.

We often let our Fear do the selecting, leaving our heart to feel the regret later. The adventure of meeting, dating, deepening and deciding is a process from which we are supposed to learn and grow. But patience does not easily grow in a garden constantly flooded with Fear.

Ultimately, I believe the comfort, happiness and security represented by the white picket fence are healthy goals. The safety and comfort we seek is a primary component of our organized society and our survival. Psychologically and emotionally we all have the need for affiliation, to be a part of a community, to belong, to love and be loved.

It is the extreme NEED to have these things totally handled (and FAST) that often clouds our choices. It is obvious that the ideal situation imagined in your teens and early twenties is most often not the same ideal image you would have in your forties. With few exceptions, we all want a happy family life, but how we define this image changes over time.

When we are young we can imagine, but we can't see. We don't yet have the experience, insight or vision to make the choices that could actually lead to a white picket fence BEYOND our dreams. With increased awareness of the pull of the white picket fence, I believe we have a better chance of not settling for the simplistic wishes of our youth simply to avoid our immediate, youthful fears.

In conclusion, there is probably little we can do to avoid the pull of the white picket fence because it is so ingrained in us as humans to seek some sort of security in our lives—and the sooner we find it, the better. Remember, this is a book of self-understanding, not self-help, but we can perhaps make better personal choices if we are aware that the white picket fence ideal is always drawing us toward it. It is a fundamentally important motivator for many of our socially influenced behaviors throughout life. Whether it's a teenager marrying their first love to live "happily ever after", or a person accepting a horrible but higher paying and more successful looking job to feel more financially secure, everyone jumps many hurdles in the rush for the "white picket fence".

Yet, what we think of as having "made it" changes for most of us throughout our lives. Safety takes on many different meanings at different life stages. The white picket fence is not a bad ideal to strive for. In fact, as we talked about in Fundamental Four, we can only contribute to others and our community when we feel safe enough to extend ourselves. But with awareness of Fundamental Five, perhaps we can leave the gate to our fence slightly ajar to allow the changing forces of Life to visit us from time to time.

FUNDAMENTAL SIX

The Immature Masculine tries to run from or dominate the Feminine.

> Behaviors you might see from OPs include: relationship partners running "hot" or loving for a while and then quickly turning cold or distant in behavior; repeated infidelities; avoidance of relational commitment; avoidance of intimate talks, physical contact or emotional expression.

Fundamental Six is the most complex of the Fundamentals to explain in any thorough way. From my experience, it is also one of the most prevalent of the many dynamics that sabotage our relationships. As with the other Fundamentals, I originally wanted to describe Fundamental Six in a short, catchy, simple way—something along the lines of "Men run from relationship commitments and their emotions." This type of explanation has worked well for some popular "relationship" authors. Unfortunately, it doesn't allow for a deeper understanding of the dynamic that causes so much trouble, pain and confusion in relationships.

To get us going through this complex fundamental, we need to understand the concepts of Feminine and Masculine that are a basic part of Fundamental Six. In a perfect world, each man and each woman would have operating within them both highly *mature* Masculine **and** Feminine forces. These forces are also referred to as "aspects" or "archetypes." Unfortunately, we do not live in a perfect world. And, unfortunately, not all of us have mature Masculine and Feminine aspects that live easily side by side in our psyches. In fact, there are all types of mature and immature Masculine and Feminine characteristics operating **within** each man and woman—and **between** each man and woman. Are you starting to feel confused yet?

Well, let's see if a little more background information will help out here.

In this Fundamental, we are not talking only about the qualities that go with the physical genders of "male" and "female." We are also focusing on internal, psychological qualities that make up our Masculine and Feminine natures. Every **man** has both psychologically Masculine and Feminine natures, and every **woman** has both psychologically Masculine and Feminine natures.

Now, this is where it gets tricky. When we take into consideration physical gender (man and woman), and psychological aspects (Masculine and Feminine), we are no longer talking about simple interactions between just a man and a woman. We are now talking about an interaction between a Man with a Masculine and a Feminine side and a Woman with a Masculine and a Feminine side. Put another way, each man has one physical and two psychological sides and each woman has one physical and two psychological sides. It's as if, we just went from a one-on-one relationship interaction to an entire crowd of interaction possibilities!

Interestingly, this multi-faceted nature—the presence of both Masculine and Feminine aspects in each individual—coincides with the anatomical structure and workings of the human brain. Each individual's brain has two hemispheres, left and right, which function very differently. In fact, their basic operating systems are opposites. The skill sets of the left and right hemispheres, as you might have guessed, coincidentally correspond to the same skill sets (qualities) of the Masculine and Feminine natures. The left hemisphere corresponds to the Masculine nature skill set and the right hemisphere corresponds to the Feminine nature skill set. (It's important to remember that we aren't talking about men and women but about the masculine and feminine natures that reside in all of us.)

Let's look at a short representative list of skill sets associated with each nature:

Masculine	Feminine
Thinking	Feeling
Linear (Black/white)	Abstract (Grey)
Numbers	Concepts
Words	Images
Goal oriented	Process oriented
Logic	Intuition
Doing	Being
Individual	Relational
Dynamic (action)	Magnetic (attraction)

As the list indicates, the corresponding words in each column are opposite poles of any chosen aspect. Neither aspect is superior to the other and each is necessary to full, mature functioning. A person in whom both natures were balanced would, in effect, "have it all". But, unfortunately, it is rare to find a person in whom these two natures are balanced.

From a development standpoint, a person becomes either Masculine-dominant or Feminine-dominant early in life—and this is not necessarily determined by gender. Some men are Feminine-dominant and some women are Masculine-dominant. So, said another way, a male body may have within it a Feminine-dominant psychology and a female body may have within it a Masculine-dominant psychology. In elementary school, Feminine dominant boys are chided by their peer-group as "sissies" or worse, and male dominant girls are labeled as "tomboys". Kids seem to have a knack for identifying these characteristics.

Let's add one more twist. The range of possible interactions between Masculine and Feminine aspects applies to same sex relationships as well as to heterosexual relationships. Again, we cannot accurately discuss the dynamics within same sex relationships by talking simply about behaviors of men and men and women and women. We must consider the complex web of possible interactions created by the influences of the internal psychological Masculine and Feminine natures. Interestingly, in enduring intimate relationships, there is usually a more Masculine dominant partner and a more Feminine dominant partner. This is true in both heterosexual relationships and homosexual relationships. Opposites, as the saying goes, apparently do attract each other, even if it appears otherwise physically.

A few real life examples may make things clearer.

Recently a client and his fiancé (let's call them Bob and Carol—not their real names) came to me for pre-marital counseling. Bob was very upset and felt like a "wimp" because he is the more emotional of the two partners. Carol is strongly driven by logic. Her appearance is somewhat masculine, and her body is very thin, with few curves to soften her look. She speaks in a tone of voice and cadence that initially reminded me of Spock on *Star Trek*.

During our sessions, Bob became emotional and cried when he spoke of his love for Carol. Carol, on the other hand, ruminated over their "potential incompatibility" due to his "asset liquidity" and the effect it might have on their "401K growth." When Bob focused on his love for Carol, he was expressing Feminine relational emotions. Carol's words, filled with numbers and references to monetary growth potentials, point to a Masculine orientation. Carol was openly aware that feeling and emotional expressions were not her strengths and also acknowledged, with some prodding, that she was really relieved that Bob is as sensitive as he is. "With him in my life now, people say that I am not as cold as I used to be—that I am a little more expressive emotionally," she said in one session. "He says the things I can't express." Bob, on the other hand, cursed his sensitivity. "Why do I have to be this way?" he would ask tearfully. "It is weak and not manly. I feel like the girl in this relationship." In truth, he is simply a Feminine dominant psychology in a male body and Carol is a Masculine dominant psychology in a female body.

Author's experience

Fundamental Six dynamics and behaviors show up in our relation-ship with ourselves as well our relationships with others. If we turn off the TV and listen to our mind chatter for a few minutes, we can hear the voices of our internal Masculine and Feminine competing for dominance. Sometimes we can hear an immature Masculine or Feminine voice chiding us from within. Anytime we say to ourselves, "Stop crying," "Stop being so emotional," or "Stop caring so much," we are experiencing some conflictual dynamic between our inner Masculine and our inner Feminine. This internal struggle between the Masculine and Feminine aspects within the individual is impacted by cultural norms, societal pressures, and good old nature and nurture influences.

Throughout recorded history there has been—and today there still is—an over-valuing of both the Masculine as a whole and of individual Masculine traits themselves. Thus, these Masculine traits are presently culturally dominant. Things that are rational, linear and scientific (Masculine) are highly praised, while things that are feeling oriented, abstract, and intuitive (Feminine) are devalued or perceived to be "weak" and "unproductive" by our current global mindset.

When I was introduced to this basic concept of Masculine/Feminine as a young psychology student, I was very curious about the repeated, successful attempts by the "Masculine" (notice I am not saying "men", although in this particular case, this might be interchangeable) to dominate or control the "Feminine." The Church did not allow Feminine figures to hold equal or important worship roles or icon status. In the U.S., until the early 1900's, most states had laws on the books that classified wives as the "property" of their husbands. Indeed, there are still a few of these laws hanging around in the world.

In our educational system, art and music classes are generally cut first when money gets tight. Math and science are more highly valued. In fact, these are the skills and areas of learning that are tested in public schools. Students are evaluated and their success measured by their mastery of Masculine skill sets while Feminine-related skill sets are considered to be "optional" or "elective." Another modern day example, the battle for Woman's Rights, is historically very recent, and although it is being fought more quietly than during its initial "hear me roar" phase, it continues today.

In trying to understand the amount of time, effort, and force expended to maintain the consistency of Masculine dominance over time, I turned to some introductory Psychology 101 principles. Remember the basic survival response to Fear—"fight or flight", which we first talked about in Fundamental One? Simply stated, we fight or flee from something or someone when we believe that its/their potential power is more powerful than ours. If something or someone is perceived to be less powerful, we are not frightened by it because we do not see how it could possibly harm us. We only squash those things that we fear might dominate us or overwhelm us in some way.

In the examples above, I see a trend that points to the existence of a "fight" response that has been successfully going on for centuries. If the power of the Feminine were not so threatening, then why would the Masculine put so much effort into, and take so many lives in the name of, destroying, dominating and controlling it? My interpretation of the evidence suggests that the Masculine consciously or unconsciously perceives the Feminine to be ultimately more powerful than it is and, therefore, it reactively attempts to control the Feminine before it becomes overpowering.

At the risk of raising the hair on the back of your neck, I will take this thought one step further. I believe that our Masculine dominated culture (including both the men **and** women who live in it) has historically feared the Feminine for so long that the fear itself has determined what form the Feminist movement has taken over the last forty years. In short, "Feminism," in the way it has been typecast and is portrayed today, looks to me a lot like "Masculinism for women." The mentality of "get a high paying job," "climb the corporate ladder," "demand higher pay and status," "career first, family and relationships last," "fight the good fight, ladies...this is war!" sounds a lot more to me like Masculine mind-think and psychology than the promotion of true Feminine values and characteristics.

I believe strongly that Feminism has been an extremely important movement for women's rights in our modern society. Yet I believe the archetypal Feminine has been so historically feared and misunderstood that it has not been accurately defended or represented by any "equality" movement up to this point in history. I believe the Masculine has dominated societies for so long that we cannot grasp a solid enough understanding of what true "feminism" (the true Feminine) looks, feels or acts like to model it differently from Masculinism. We are too influenced by the long reign of the Masculine to create a new, unbiased vision of the Feminine. In short, we as a culture are so consciously and unconsciously ingrained in the Masculine perspective, that even our culture's Feminism looks Masculine.

Please understand, in talking about the Feminine, I am not discussing Women's Rights. Personally, I believe that women should have all rights equal to those of men. Rather, I am presenting my perspectives on the psychological Masculine and Feminine in men and women. If we look at the historical reaction to and treatment of Feminine aspects, it appears to me that the Feminine is, using basic 101 Psychology principles, inherently viewed to be more powerful than the Masculine. The Masculine unconsciously (and sometimes consciously) knows this, is threatened by it, and therefore has gone to great lengths to subdue, dominate and control the Feminine.

Now that I have cleared that up and hopefully avoided a good bit of hate mail, let's get back to Fundamental Six. To start understanding at a deeper level how the dynamics catalyzed by this Fundamental show up in our lives, let's get more familiar with the personality and qualities of the Masculine aspect, which, by the way, has been getting some very unflattering "press" over the past couple of decades.

Healthy vs. Immature Masculine

I believe fully that the Masculine, at individual and collective levels, can develop into a mature healthy aspect that enriches our lives and relationships, and that protects the creative, tender Feminine inside each of us. It is the Immature Masculine that has the primary negative impact on relationship dynamics. But before we discuss these impacts, let's talk about the vision of the Healthy Masculine and contrast it with the Immature Masculine.

The Healthy Masculine's primary function is to protect the Feminine and to provide physical and psychological safety and security to those around it. When we act on the instinctual urge to come to the rescue of another person, the Healthy Masculine is flying his colors. People who have developed a Healthy Masculine often become "Good Samaritans" and find themselves in the middle of conflicts involving an endangered stranger before they even know what came over them. If a Healthy Masculine has been developed within the individual, the "warrior" will come forward when there is danger to one's self or another. He will even leap forth from someone who never before thought of themselves as brave. The Healthy Masculine cannot resist helping someone in genuine need or danger. You may ask, "But what about that powerful maternal instinct of a mother to protect her children at all costs?" I call this the "momma bear" instinct. Woe be unto anyone caught by a momma bear if they are hurting her cubs. While this is a powerful instinct, I am separating maternal instinct (Feminine) from warrior instinct (Masculine). Maternal instinct specifically involves protecting family members. Warrior instinct, on the other hand, shows up as a general drive to protect anyone in danger and can be experienced by both men and women.

Within the individual, the Healthy Masculine can show up as a natural instinct to protect our own limits and boundaries. Someone who has developed a Healthy Masculine within can say "No" and will not let himself or herself "go too far", so to speak. The Healthy Masculine knows when "enough is enough," and will not push itself, or allow others to push it, to a point of real psychological, emotional or physical danger. Yet, the Healthy Masculine is not afraid of expressing a full range of emotions or entering into committed relationships because he is confident of his ability to protect himself in most situations. The Healthy Masculine can stand before a crowd with tears of deep emotion in his eyes and project a deep sense of power without evoking pity. He never falls pray to "victim-hood" and does not give his power away by playing "poor me." He communicates authentically and doesn't attack others unfairly or behind their backs. The Healthy Masculine engages conflict directly, and does not randomly create conflicts and then leave the situation for others to sort out. It is important to remember here that both men and women can display this type of Healthy Masculine.

The Immature Masculine, on the other hand, is an entirely different animal. Picture a thirteen or fourteen-year-old boy and how he acts and reacts to the world. This is a pretty accurate depiction of the Immature Masculine. Now think of that same fourteen-year-old boy around a girl that he likes and watch the dynamics between them. Notice how he can barely get his words to come out. Since he cannot express himself verbally, he tends to roughhouse physically with the girl, punching her in the arm if too much silent time goes by.

There is a wonderful scene in the movie *Risky Business* that visually shows this dynamic so clearly. In one short snippet, a teenage boy is sitting alone on a sofa. After a few moments, two beautiful adult women come in and sit on either side of him. They silently wait for him to talk to them. It only takes a few seconds for their presence to become overwhelming to the teenager and he gets up from the sofa and leaves the room grinning, without saying a word. This is a typical reaction of the Immature Masculine when it is around the mature Feminine. If he does not avoid the situation by running to another activity (as shown in this example), he will most likely punch, poke or ridicule the female to relieve his tension and awkwardness.

The movie *My Fair Lady* is another great example of the Immature Masculine and how it deals with the Feminine. The movie captured for me the difficulties the Masculine has in understanding the Feminine. Professor Higgins, played by Rex Harrison, involves himself with an experiment to change Liza Doolittle, played by Audrey Hepburn, from a poor flower girl into a refined woman of society. By the end of the movie, it is truly he who is transformed, while she is merely unwrapped. He struggles with her effect on him and sings a song entitled, *"Why can't a woman be more like a man,"* which tells of his desire to be in relationship with her **and** the frustration he encounters as he tries to figure out how to go about the whole process. Another song from the movie, "*I will never let a woman in my life*," shows the natural defensiveness the Masculine has to the Feminine and its uniquely different mode of operating.

As the movie draws to a close, Professor Higgins realizes he loves Eliza and he cannot find peace without her. But he is unwilling to admit this to her directly. The Immature Masculine must pretend it is the more powerful force in the relationship in order to compensate for the opposite fact that it is NOT the more powerful of the two forces. When Liza returns to him in the end because of her own love, he greets her presence first with a secret look of relief and then the bellicose order, "FETCH my slippers!" The entire movie shows the struggle of the Immature Masculine as it attempts to deal with and relate to the presence of the Feminine. Initially it must demean her, pretending she has no value. When she begins to have a restorative and vitalizing effect on him, he must both fight and ignore the positive effects she is having on him.

Unfortunately the Immature Masculine is more prevalent in our culture than the Healthy Masculine. In "adult" relationships (remember, Immature Masculine traits are not present **just** in young people), the Immature Masculine avoids conflict or any discussion involving problems in the relationship. It avoids vulnerable feelings, usually relates socially with only a small circle of superficial buddies, dreads "unknown" gatherings, and generally prefers isolation and set routines. You might note these are also characteristics we can easily use to describe our fourteen-year-old friend.

I have personally and professionally witnessed another example that typifies the Immature Masculine: the male who "disappears" from his family every weekend by watching T.V. sports all day and all night. (I am sure that there are Masculine dominant women who do something similar. I just haven't seen them in my practice.) The ignored female partner will often go crazy for a while trying to pry her male partner away from the T.V. She may resort to picking fights to get her partner's attention and to coerce him into participating in shared social activities. After a while, the female partner usually gives up the struggle and begins building a social life without her mate, leaving her male partner alone to watch his sports.

I believe this is an extreme, but all too prevalent, example of the stereotypical Immature Masculine attempting to avoid relationship conflicts with his mate and family. Ultimately, he may be avoiding situations in which he might be asked to express feelings. Now, watching weekend sports events is not **always** an avoidant behavior. I love to watch my college teams play on Saturdays. But the Immature Masculine can use sports activities as an easy excuse to avoid relating emotionally for **large and long** blocks of time because it is an activity that precludes other more relational activities—like talking. There is a marked difference between watching several games during the weekend and disappearing for the WHOLE weekend, every weekend.

The immature masculine can also be seen when the wife complains that the husband "doesn't pay attention to her," seems emotionally distant except when he wants sex, and avoids any talk about relationship issues and problems. When confronted with the dreaded words, "We need to talk," the husband may say, mostly to himself, "Talk? Talk? Didn't we just talk six months ago?" By the time the couple gets to my office, things have usually deteriorated so badly that the husband shows up just to avoid losing the marriage.

Another form of the immature masculine is seen in situations where a female client complains that her male partner is very loving and affectionate to her for a period of time and then freakishly, without warning, turns cold and distant. Everything seems to be going fine and then, BOOM, out of the blue, the male starts shutting down emotionally. When he is asked about his sudden change in behavior or emotional expression, he either denies it or says he is just "tired" or "stressed."

A third example of the immature masculine can be seen when the "male" aspect of one person feverishly pursues the "female" aspect of another person until the couple marries. After they get married the "male" interior aspect of the pursuer then turns emotionally unavailable, causing an uncomfortable distance between the couple throughout the relationship. Variations of this dynamic also occur in friendships and other relationships: (1) one person primarily or always initiates "getting together" and the other is "too busy" or unavailable, or (2) one person consistently does nice things to help out the other and the kindness is ignored, unacknowledged or unappreciated, and not returned.

Many readers may find that at least one of these examples sounds familiar as they frequently appear in relationships and are apparent to those who are psychologically aware.

So, why does the Immature Masculine work so hard to avoid interactions that may promote emotional interchange? Remember our earlier discussion about the concept that the Feminine is emotionally and psychologically perceived to be more powerful than the Masculine? Well, imagine the Immature Masculine feeling dominated by the mere presence of the Feminine in the same room. If their mere presence is threatening, why then would the masculine want to interact **verbally** with the "feared enemy?" The Immature Masculine feels incapable of saying "no" to any demand put forth by the Feminine or at at the very least, feels very guilty if he does say "no." In order to avoid refusing a demand, he must come up with a plan.

Remaining silent in this situation actually seems like a very smart move. Rather than inviting an interactive situation, wouldn't it feel better to skulk away and "disappear" in front of the T.V. to watch "manly" activities that reinforce masculine strength and isolation? If the Immature Masculine can "look busy" in front of the T.V., it is **less likely** to get "called out" to "talk" or be forced to go to some social function it has no interest in attending. Try to get a typical fourteen-year-old boy to either talk about his feelings or to go to a social function and you will get to visually see the resistance and power struggle the inner Immature Masculine goes through in an attempt to insulate itself! In this context, the television set may be an electronic emotional escape mechanism—and perhaps one of the last remaining "cave dwellings" in which the modern Immature Masculine can seek shelter.

Exercising and actually participating in sports may be other safe havens, as we will see in the example below.

"Here she is, Kevin, the only woman I ever wanted this badly. She is perfect in every way for me. She exercises, she is smart, she's gorgeous, everybody likes her and I get home and it's like, I just shut down. I walk in the door, barely say hi to her, put on my running clothes and I'm out the door for my hour jog. It's like I have to get out of there FAST. So I'm jogging and my mind shuts down so I don't have to think about what I just did and when I get home she starts asking me questions about my day and stuff and I'm just thinking 'shut up already!' 'Shut up and leave me alone!' I'm thinking all this and I love her. I love her more than anything and I just want her to **not** talk. Just be there, but don't talk. It's like a conversation would just kill me or something.

I ask myself why I can't just answer her questions and tell her how I feel and all—-and I've got no good answer to that. It's like I am so sure that she is so much better than me, so much smarter, that if I can just hide somehow until the next morning, we can go to work and it will be all right again. I just wish we could go to work, and do our little social events together, but just not have to talk to each other while we're doing it.

So what do I do? I shut her down as soon as I can. I criticize every little thing she does. Nothing meets my standards...it's not clean enough, food's overcooked, she could lose a few pounds, whatever, I just shut her down so she won't talk to me for a while. I hate myself while I am doing it, but I just won't stop.

From actual conversation

To take another look at the reactions of an activated and suspicious Immature Masculine, have you ever wondered why men hate it so much when women cry? In that moment of raw emotion, the Immature Masculine is overwhelmed. When the "woman" (Feminine) cries, the "man" (Masculine) first feels guilty, and then gets angry because he doesn't know how to "fix" the problem that has created the tears.

Once again, the Immature Masculine responds much like the over-stressed fourteen-year-old who lashes out when he doesn't know how to handle a situation.

In general, avoidance is the main behavioral defense mechanism utilized by the Immature Masculine, whether it shows up as avoidance of commitment, physical affection or intimacy. Have you ever wondered why a lover rolls away from his/her partner after sex? This is another reaction of the threatened Immature Masculine. In fact, the Immature Masculine may find it unbearable to stay physically connected to their lover after sex. Why? Remember, once again, how they feel overwhelmed in the presence of the Feminine in another person? Imagine how they feel when the very nature of the sexual contact causes a relational connection—a dropping of the distance and the armoring that the Immature Masculine is so good at hiding behind.

This dropping of armor allows a person's Feminine side (feelings) to spring forth from its internal jail cell. In this vulnerable state, the Immature Masculine can feel those dreaded emotions it has armored itself against. If you thought the Immature Masculine felt vulnerable and threatened **before** sex, after sex it is dealing with two Feminine natures: their partners **and** theirs! The easiest and quickest solution to this discomfort is to leave, emotionally or physically, after sex. Physical distance is an instrument of false security that the Immature Masculine uses to protect itself from feelings of vulnerability, both within itself and in relation to others.

This same dynamic explains why certain people endlessly push for more closeness in a relationship (moving from casual dating to going steady, getting engaged or married, or moving in together) and then become emotionally cold or unavailable when they reach that goal. The Immature Masculine doesn't want to be totally alone. In fact, it loves to have company (preferably in the form of buddies). This desire for a buddy sometimes compels the Immature Masculine to push forward in a relationship.

But, soon the Immature Masculine runs up against a conflict. It really only wants to engage in relationships on its own terms and conditions, usually using what is called the "Buddy Code." The "Buddy Code", simply stated, says, *"We get together when we get together with no obligations or notifications required. We see each other when we see each other, no plans are necessary, and no bitching or emotional outbursts about the lack of plans or notification is allowed."* Because the Immature Masculine is both terrified of being alone **and** of being emotionally involved, it is continually haunted by these two opposing fears. It becomes terrified during the process of bonding and runs for the nearest cover (i.e. the T.V. or to the gym) to hide. The Immature Masculine is literally damned if it is alone and damned if it is relationally connected. The best solution for this dilemma is maturation.

The Healthy Masculine is not driven by these fears. It is secure in its ability to say "no" to the Feminine without feeling guilty. The lack of guilt is an important distinction because, while the Immature Masculine can say "no" and does so very often, it then pays an emotional price in the form of guilt. The guilt the Immature Masculine feels when is says "no" to the Feminine is much like the guilt one feels when one says "no" to one's mother. It is a guilt that is also connected to the fear of survival. The Immature Masculine does not want to feel this residual, internal guilt, so it avoids the possibility of receiving a request as often as it can. Remember the fourteen-year-old boy? He will often disappear when there is work to be done or chores to be completed. Similarly, the Immature Masculine in adult males will cause men to mysteriously disappear when there is relationship work to be done.

The Healthy Masculine, to the contrary, is perfectly capable of saying "no" to requests without feeling guilty and can stay present to negotiate a compromise, if needed. He does not need to avoid interactions with the Feminine. Actually, the Healthy Masculine finds the Feminine absolutely invigorating and inspiring and greatly enjoys her company. He also enjoys being alone because his alone time has a very different quality to it than time spent with the Feminine. This occasional alone time is always a choice and not a forced reaction, defense or avoidance behavior.

As mentioned earlier, we each have both internal Masculine and Feminine aspects that are interacting and encountering conflicts within our individual psyches. Even when we are alone, there is interplay between these polarities going on all the time inside of us. For example, people, most notably men, in our Western culture often struggle with their internal emotionality (Feminine nature) in social situations. By contrast, in some European cultures, crying and other displays of emotion among men are openly accepted and encouraged as signs of strength and connectedness. These European men who freely express their emotions are seen as passionate and strong, not weak and "womanly."

This acceptance is obviously not true in the Western world, and especially in the U.S. Our cultural norms create a certain amount of pressure on men to deny the Feminine aspect that lives inside of them. One of my biggest fears during my teenage years was that I would cry in public when I was in a movie theatre. I considered this to be a fate worse than death. This created a problem because I felt my emotions very deeply and was susceptible to shedding tears more than many boys my age. It was only in my thirties that I finally stopped squelching my emotions in theatres. But you would be surprised how many times I have left theatres with eyes red from crying and noticed perfect strangers pointing and snickering at me. Can you guess the usual age range and gender of these strangers? You guessed it— teenage boys. Since I have personally experienced this ridicule, I take special care to point out to my clients that when their emotions are singled out or ridiculed, it is always the Immature Masculine in others that is reacting because it is threatened by others' emotional displays.

Again, the insecurity and discomfort felt around expressing emotions is not a dynamic experienced only between men and women in relationship to others. It can also be experienced *within* an individual. I have witnessed women and men who are dominated by an Immature Masculine demean **themselves** verbally when they cry unexpectedly. One female client in particular had a habit of spontaneously crying while talking and then saying in a bitter, angry tone under her breath, "Why am I crying…(pause)…(angrily)…how stupid…it's just plain stupid…I am so stupid," while she wiped the current tears away and continued fighting back new ones. This is the voice of the Immature Masculine who is overwhelmed by the healthy display of emotion (Feminine nature) within this woman.

Whenever the Immature Masculine experiences any emotion other than anger (which is the only emotion it is comfortable with because it lacks the quality of vulnerability), it basically "freaks out" and either gets angry (fights) or runs (flees). It feels it should "do something" in the presence of emotion and, since it doesn't know what to do, it falls back on the instinctive "fight or flight" reaction.

The Healthy Masculine can stand silently and comfortably in the middle of an emotional outburst or scene and not feel overwhelmed in the moment. The Healthy Masculine trusts that it can handle whatever is needed, if a need arises. It maintains its presence and simply remains available physically (to give hugs and physical contact) and emotionally (to just listen or be a sounding board). The Immature Masculine desperately pushes the emotional person toward some solution, any solution (requested or not). The Healthy Masculine simply listens patiently. The Immature Masculine impatiently says, "Things will get better, don't cry, now let's go eat." The Healthy Masculine empathizes and says, "That must be awful," and sits down and continues to listen.

Individuals who are dealing with heavy emotions and have a developed Healthy Masculine, can stay present, feel the entirety and depth of the emotion, and even process those emotions more fully to reach an understanding of the situation without judging the process as "stupid" or "weak." The process is not viewed as dangerous and something to be avoided. It is simply viewed as what it truly is: a healthy connection to the Feminine and a healthy release of emotion. This is the way things naturally unfold when one has a healthy, balanced flow within one's own psyche.

Finally, the most disturbing and dangerous aspect of the Immature Masculine, I believe, is its potential to react violently when it is threatened and/or feels too overwhelmed. If the Immature Masculine finds itself in a threatening situation that it cannot easily escape, or that brings up a degree of emotion that the underdeveloped psyche cannot handle, the Immature Masculine will resort to the only skills it knows at the time that will protect it—or remove it—from the threat. Generally, the coping skills fall into two familiar categories: fight or flight. If the Immature Masculine is dominant in a person, when it feels "cornered" it is likely that this person will resort to physical force to feel safe or to protect itself. Because of this, I believe the Immature Masculine is the psychological root of domestic abuse and much of the relational violence we see in the world today.

There is some good news in this theory. If we help the Immature Masculine develop more mature skills and broaden its range of behavioral choices, the habit of reacting with violence to threatening situations can be broken. I believe it is psychological laziness that causes repeated acts of violence. Those who are willing to improve themselves can develop alternatives to using violence as a defense against vulnerability and overwhelming feelings.

While relationships between individuals reflect the majority of the ways this Fundamental plays out, there are also groups and entire industries that are ruled by it. Two major industries that are dominated by characteristics of the Immature Masculine are Hollywood and the modeling industry. Surprising as this may sound, both industries are still Masculine-dominated and are therefore prone to an Immature Masculine perspective in their view of what is acceptable or "bankable." The most obvious reflection of the Immature Masculine is the overwhelming number of super skinny female models and actors that represent the industry standard of beauty.

Why would this be true? Remember, the Immature Masculine is threatened by all things Feminine, and therefore must (consciously or unconsciously) dominate or avoid every expression of the Feminine. What physical body type, then, would be acceptable or considered beautiful to the Immature Masculine? You guessed it: anything NOT Feminine in physical nature, which means NO CURVES. Curves are characteristic of the Feminine, so they instinctively repel the Immature Masculine. The skinnier the better—always! Female actors that even approach normal weight for their height are rejected every day as "too fat." "Lose weight, lose weight, lose weight," is the mantra heard by models and actors within these industries on a daily basis. The less curves the better, because curves naturally represent the Feminine and therefore are threatening to the Immature Masculine.

Those readers who are staring at this page in a "deer in the headlights" mode, should take heart. I am going to pull together all of the ground we have covered in this Fundamental.

While reading through Fundamental Six, you may have noticed that it is really an extension of Fundamental One (Everyone is terrified...). Actually, it is a detailed and applied explanation of a specific kind of Fear that arises within each of us, and between us, because of the interplay of Masculine and Feminine archetypes.

If you take a minute to sit back and absorb what you have read so far, you may begin to see the less obvious but numerous extensions of Fundamental One within this Fundamental. With some reflection, you may be able to see how Fear in its endless permutations affects very specific areas of our lives. If you take the basics of Fundamental Six and apply them to corporations, social groups, cultures and even countries, you might easily find ways these dynamics affect your marriage, your family, your neighborhood or even world events.

Hopefully, it will make you more aware of the Masculine and Feminine aspects that battle or negotiate daily inside of you, and open the door to a broader range of possibilities that can be developed to enhance your relationships with yourself and others.

FUNDAMENTAL SEVEN

Everyone points the finger.

> Behaviors you might see from OPs include: heavy judgment/
> anger toward others or their actions; lack of empathy/
> understanding of others' hardships, lifestyles or way of
> life; heavy righteousness around one's own opinions and
> lifestyle; expecting others to live by behaviors that you
> yourself do not live by; believing that everyone else "has
> the problem", not you; ability to totally "write off" friends
> or relatives for one perceived "bad" or inappropriate act or
> situation.

Let's start this chapter off with a visual-aid that you can supply for
yourself at home. First take your hand and point at something. Do
that right now. Now look at the hand you are pointing with. See how
the index finger is pointing forward, but the three fingers under-
neath it are pointing toward you? When I was younger, I remember
being amused when someone said that when you point your finger
at someone in judgement, remember that there are three fingers
pointing back at you. I did not fully appreciate what this meant at the
time, but it interested me because I felt there was some deeper truth
to the statement, if I could only grasp it. While Fundamental Seven
is one of the simplest to describe (it doesn't get much simpler than a
pointing finger), it is one of the most difficult to truly take to heart.

And, if you do take it to heart, it is probably the most personally threatening of the Fundamentals. Why? Because it challenges us to look within ourselves when it would be much easier to look away. This Fundamental also holds within it the secret to one of the craziest things people do every day: cause traffic problems because they just **have** to slow down to look at wrecks. More on that later.

The easiest way to approach Fundamental Seven is to begin with an assumption that it is human nature to want to look our best at all times. Although few people will truly live up to this goal, most people desire it, nonetheless. This desire to "look good" includes both looking great on both the outside and the inside. People who look good on the outside get a lot of attention and have more opportunities, just because they are "pretty" or "handsome." In addition to that, we all wish to be perceived as "good do-bees" who have nothing but good, goody, goodness radiating from within our gorgeous exteriors. As you may well already know from experience, true, pure goodness is rare, but we sure seem to enjoy trying hard to make it look as if we possess it.

Since the desire to look and to act beautifully is a primary goal for most of us, what do we do with the fact that some of our aspects are frankly downright ugly? The answer is easy. We try to pretend that those parts do not exist. "Those ugly parts are just not mine, thank you very much. Nope, others may look that way/have those issues/do that horrible thing/think that terrible thought about others, but not **me**. I am just practically perfect in every way."

We avoid and fear (back to Fundamental One again) seeing these not-so-pretty aspects of ourselves so intensely that we often repress any knowledge of them and avoid looking at them. Remember the tape recording played at the beginning of each segment of the old Mission Impossible television show? The voice on the tape reminded the agent that if any of the team members were caught or killed, the Secretary would disavow any knowledge of their identity. Well, in this case, the tape from the little voice inside of us might say, "As usual, if any aspects of your ugly side are seen or pointed out to you, your conscious mind will disavow any knowledge of their existence."

"I've just finished planning the 50th birthday party of my new girlfriend of one year. We are in New York and I reserved the entire restaurant for all our friends to celebrate. I have been divorced for over a year and I have two children. I share custody with my ex-wife. I left my wife two years ago because she was, it turned out, a hopeless crack cocaine addict. I found out later that she used to bring her drug dealers over to the apartment when I was at work to do drugs and God knows what else…this all while my children were there! She should never have gotten shared custody, but that's the law for you. Anyway I had been fighting with my ex for weeks prior to the party and she had been calling all the time, I think just to make it harder for me to plan the party she knew was coming up because like an idiot, I told her.

Okay, night of the party, we are all dressed up and ready to go…KNOCK-KNOCK at the door. 7:30 P.M. It is a guy with a court injunction saying Lisa, my girlfriend, cannot be in the same house as HER (my ex's) children because Lisa would be a bad influence on them because we are not married and blah, blah, blah. Lisa is a well-respected pediatrician in New York and this crack addict, ex-wife of mine, is calling HER a bad influence on our kids. And she really believed that too. She was totally indignant later in front of the judge, like she was some paragon of virtue. I thought it was an act at first, but she truly thought my girlfriend would ruin my children!"

From actual conversation

You see, others around us recognize and have to deal with our undesirable aspects, habits and behavioral quirks every day. We may believe that we are successfully hiding these aspects—but they are not invisible at all. Our own unattractive aspects are simply invisible to **us**. Interestingly, while these unpleasant aspects are "consciously" invisible to us, our **unconscious** mind is very aware of them. In fact, full knowledge of all aspects of our nature—good and bad—are stored in our unconscious.

The unconscious mind is the closet where knowledge of our unpleasant aspects is tucked away until the conscious mind brings them to awareness. These traits that we would most likely label as "undesirable" are parts of us that lie waiting in a sort of "lost and found" holding pattern, until one day they are claimed by our conscious mind and integrated into our conscious awareness of Self.

Unfortunately, until these unpleasant aspects are "found" (brought to consciousness), they remain "lost" (ignored). If they remain "lost", we cannot improve ourselves fully as human beings. We cannot work on something that we cannot see or refuse to acknowledge. This principle can be simply stated: Everything we acknowledge about ourselves we can change. Anything we ignore or deny about ourselves we cannot change.

Let me assert here my belief that every human being over time moves toward some improvement or personal discovery, even if they seem to fight this movement throughout their life. It seems that moving forward along the path of personal evolution is part of the "Divine Plan." In an attempt to help us grow as human beings, the unconscious mind leaks out these important, unknown aspects of ourselves from time to time, allowing us, willingly or unwillingly, to explore them and to work on them. Our unconscious mind does not mean to rub our noses in all this. It just allows them to come out of hiding in little dribs and drabs. If we show even the least bit of curiosity, this interest opens up a fortunate opportunity for us to gain more knowledge of our deeper selves.

Here is where the pointing finger comes into play. Let's use aggressive driving as an example. Say you are an aggressive driver, but you generally do not see yourself in this light. Although people tell you all the time that you drive like a maniac or that driving with you is like riding a roller coaster, you write off those comments by saying they are just the opinions of wimpy drivers or wimpy passengers. Your unconscious mind knows that you are an aggressive driver, but you deny it to yourself. This unacknowledged truth keeps simmering inside of you until so much steam or energy builds up around it, that it must be released.

The built-up energy literally raises your finger and causes you to point to someone else and scream: "Look at that aggressive driver over there! With the way he drives, he is going to kill someone!"

You have just committed a textbook example of Fundamental Seven behavior. You have just "pointed the finger." Although almost everyone may notice bad driving by others, the WORST drivers point out bad driving more often than good driving. They usually will express the most anger (and other emotions!) when they deliver their accusation.

To recap, everyone points the finger because the unconscious mind is constantly leaking out manifestations of our own unconscious aspects, which we don't want to claim. Because these aspects are too uncomfortable to directly acknowledge about ourselves, we project them onto someone else. In other words, since you cannot acknowledge the behavior in yourself, you project the behavior (like showing a movie through a projector) onto the nearest "screen." In the example above, the screen was the aggressive driver who crossed your path. If there are people in the car with you when you point your finger and scream about "that crazy driver," they will probably laugh and say, "Yea, that is exactly what we say about how you drive." You will ignore them and think they are either wrong or exaggerating. **They** can see your behavior. You cannot.

Another common example of this phenomenon often happens when you run into a friend to whom you have not talked in a long while. When you unexpectedly run into each other, they say in a scolding tone, "Why don't you ever call me? I never hear from you?" I am personally fascinated when this happens to me because it is so obvious that the person pointing the finger is forgetting the obvious. If **neither** of you has talked for a while, then **they** haven't been calling you either! You are equally guilty—but they seem to want to blame **you**. It is a common example of projection—the person who is pointing the finger at you is guilty of the same behavior, but is not taking responsibility for it.

"We had this family friend, Leonard, father of eight children that I would see maybe once a year. He worked in the same plant as my father for thirty years. When my father died, he knew Dad was no stellar character or father to me and he also knew when I saw him that I had gotten an important job and was starting the next day. I was like eighteen at the time and he started in on this advice to me out of the blue.

'Bob,' he said, 'Don't turn out like your Dad, don't limp in to your new job, you need to stand up straight with both hands open for whatever they give you. Honesty, that is the only **way** to be—you gotta stand up straight in every way, stand up straight,' he said hunching over in some mocking imitation, I guess, of how he saw my Dad when he worked with him.

Now I never saw my Dad at work, but I liked the 'stand up straight' expression...it sort of said something to me. Leonard seemed to take great pleasure in pointing out my Dad's faults and went on and on about 'stand up straight' and 'give them your best days work everyday' and 'honesty is the only policy'. We laughed because he sounded like a broken record repeating those three lines while walking hunched over and laughing all the while. He seemed so sincere, and I didn't take insult in him telling me not to be like my Dad—I wasn't that big a fan of Dad myself. He openly disapproved of my Dad's less than honest ways, I didn't ask specifics, but he was right, in most ways my Dad never 'stood up straight'.

I liked Leonard for his advice; he seemed like an honest, caring man. I always respected him after that day—-and that was the last time I ever saw him. Get this, years later I ran into another coworker of Leonard and my Dad's and asked about Leonard because I knew he was getting up in age. This guy told me that Leonard got fired before his retirement, because, get this, the guy says, 'Listen I know your Dad and Leonard were friends and your Dad had his problems like the rest of us, but he did a good job everyday—not like Leonard.'

I'm like, 'What?'

He says, 'Leonard was known around the planet as the laziest, slowest, worker there was. He did the least amount possible and tried to stay out sick once a week for this or that injury. Union's what kept him his job for years, but he finally got fired—for stealing toilet paper.'

I looked at him shocked.

'Yea,' he continued. 'He lost retirement for stealing that shitty ass plant toilet paper that I would try not to use even when I was at work. It wasn't even worth stealing, but he lost his retirement over it.' He kind of laughed and said, 'Lazy and dishonest is not a good combination for work.' I was stunned.

From actual conversation

Fundamental Seven behaviors do not just occur at the individual level. As you read this, countries, political and religious leaders and even business organizations across the world are pointing at others' behaviors and characteristics and judging them as "terrible" or immoral." If we are on the receiving end of the pointing finger, we could very easily turn these accusations around and find examples of these same behaviors and characteristics in our accusers. When an individual or group projects their unacknowledged "parts" onto others, the "pointer" either becomes overly angry at the "pointee" or—at the most basic level, just "hates" them. Here is a dramatic example: I once worked with a manager who would constantly go into a tirade about the "crooks" he used to work for at his previous company. "Those @#$%# crooks," he would almost scream, "are ripping people off left and right!" When he resigned a couple of years later, his secretary told us about the many ways he used to cheat our company out of money and the numerous conversations she had with him to encourage him to stop engaging in corporate theft.

Other examples include:

- People who feel ugly physically but don't want to acknowledge it will often viciously point-out all the "ugly" people they see. This is a common phenomenon in teenagers who are hypercritical during their teenage "awkward" phase.

- People who are "show-offs" or are overly needy will point out or hate "attention getters" of any kind. They often avoid being around children as a group because the children's (age- appropriate) high need for attention reflects their own high-attention needs.

- Extremely vain people will hate actors or people they perceive as "primpers" or "posers."

- People with repressed sexual desires or secret sex lives will hate "sluts" and "sinners" or the "sexually depraved".

One of my favorite variations of this last example is something I see personally and professionally all the time: the sexually promiscuous partner who is ragefully jealous and/or hyper-controlling of their non-promiscuous partner. The most common example of this is the super controlling male who accuses his girlfriend or wife of flirting with other men. This is the guy who won't let "his woman" out of his sight, allow her to spend time with friends away from him, or permit her to wear anything even slightly attractive out in public. Whenever I see a man who is super controlling with his partner, I know one of two things: either he is on the bottom rung of the self-esteem ladder when it comes to his relationship, or he is having an affair, or feels urges to have one…or both. He is "projecting" his own bad behavior or urges onto his partner.

Sometimes an aspect being judged by someone is so deeply hidden inside the person pointing the finger that others would never suspect that the judged trait is alive and well inside the judger. For example, I have seen some burly men declare they hate "bleeding heart, liberal, cry babies." Then, in a therapeutic session, they will surprise me by repeatedly expressing deeply tender, emotional sides of themselves. They might angrily call other men wimps and yet unexpectedly sob at the sight of a dead squirrel lying by the side of the road. There is another very important point to be made here: it is not just traits that are perceived to be negative that make a person uncomfortable enough to hide or deny them. Genuinely positive traits can evoke a person's discomfort as well.

As illustrated in the last example, the burly man negatively judged emotional sensitivity and thus hated it in other men. By most standards, emotional sensitivity is not a negative trait, but this man judged it to be so because he was uncomfortable with his own feeling side. His perception was also influenced by his male peer group, which generally sees emotional sensitivity as a weakness. In reality, balanced sensitivity is a very positive aspect. But since it is not perceived to be positive by "them," they hate it in others. Thus begins the finger pointing.

Adolescent boys often call a boy in their group a "sissy" or a "wimp" if they see him cry. Yet they are privately very sensitive themselves. The "tougher" boys just fight harder to avoid their feelings than the boys who express their emotions. Because they feel threatened by a crying boy's sensitivity, they point the finger.

Now, let's turn our attention to the opposite side of the finger pointing coin. As I mentioned earlier, just as people will point the finger at others who display their unacknowledged negative traits, they will also point the finger at others who embody positive traits they do not acknowledge about themselves. Why, you ask, would people not recognize or acknowledge their positive traits? Well, sometimes positive psychological or physical traits can be "simply too much" for the individual to acknowledge about themselves because of their level of self-esteem. For example, very talented people often point the finger at other equally talented people and wish they were as "gifted." Friends who witness this "wishing and hoping" will often respond immediately with, "What? Are you crazy? Your work is just as good—if not better—than theirs!" But often the person who acknowledges their gift in others cannot see the similar greatness in their own work or presence.

I have personally and professionally witnessed very beautiful women wistfully point their fingers at **other** women they felt were truly beautiful. While they could acknowledge the other women for their beauty, they could not recognize and accept their own. Instead, they projected "beauty" onto others with their pointing finger. When someone positively points the finger at another, it is usually done without jealousy. My experience is that in these circumstances, the finger is gently pointed with a true sense of respect and awe and not as a manipulative maneuver to evoke a compliment. The strength of the positive aspect within the projecting person may just be too overwhelming for their ego to handle in relation to themselves.

Interestingly, the Masculine tends to act differently in the positive finger-pointing arena than the Feminine. Gender-difference studies have shown that women generally have more trouble taking full credit for their achievements than men do. Women tend to attribute their achievements to luck or good fortune, while men usually attribute their successes to their own intelligence and hard work. Many women find it "simply too much" to take credit for the talents, hard work, determination, creativity and just plain "smarts" that are responsible for their achievements. Thus, they downplay their own successes and "project" their success onto others around them, who may or may not deserve the praise.

Men, on the other hand, will not only take full credit for what they have personally accomplished, but they will often give themselves credit for what they did **not** actually accomplish. This difference reflects my belief that people with innately higher levels of self-confidence are less likely to power-grab for credit. It seems people with a good bit of inner strength and confidence do not seem to consistently fight over trivial matters. Trivialities, like taking personal credit, do not appear to be important enough for truly gifted people to fight over.

Now that we have looked at the basic reasons for Fundamental Seven finger pointing, let's look at how this Fundamental influences our own behaviors and our relationships with others. Basically, Fundamental Seven suggests that everything you are judging negatively or positively in others, is probably also something **you** have done, felt, or thought of, consciously or unconsciously. In my experience, there is a marked difference between negative finger pointing and objective observance, which is a healthy activity. The difference is the presence of a strong emotion—usually anger. People who are objectively pointing out an aspect they are observing in another are usually not raging or raising their voices when they verbalize their observations.

They are simply pointing something out. The negative "pointing finger" is usually accompanied by some intense emotion, which represents the "steam" this unacknowledged aspect is creating inside the pointer's unconscious mind. If and when the previously unknown aspect finally does come forward into the pointer's conscious awareness, only then can they recognize and accept what is happening. It is only through this understanding that this "steam" can be released in a productive way.

There are added benefits to allowing our unconscious traits to become conscious. Once we become conscious of an aspect, especially a negative one, we are always more compassionate toward others displaying the same aspect. Rather than pointing our fingers at them in anger, we begin to reach out our hand to them in understanding. Rather than self righteously rejecting a characteristic, we begin to embrace the defense mechanisms that cemented it in place. The pointing finger, then, is ultimately a pathway toward human development if we know how to interpret it correctly and learn to use it as a tool.

Unfortunately, most people would rather take the easy way out. They choose to negatively judge someone rather than taking the more humble approach of looking inside themselves and saying, "At one time or another I have done or thought something like that myself." We see the blaming, unconstructive use of the pointing finger in politics all the time. One party accuses the party currently in power of a wrongdoing that they themselves engaged in during the years when they were in power. It is perceived to be easier in the moment to look blameless and to judge others than it is to be humble and honest. This defensiveness is, unfortunately, an ingrained part of human nature. But, without breaking the finger pointing cycle, and adopting a new perspective based on humility and acceptance, people will continue to do some seemingly crazy, crazy things motivated by the hidden parts of their unconscious.

Oh, by the way. I haven't forgotten about the car wreck question presented at the beginning of this chapter. Have you ever wondered why people just HAVE to slow down to look at wrecks on the side of the road or police cars that have their lights flashing? Why do people seem incapable of simply driving by an accident without gawking and slowing down to a crawl? Have you ever noticed how hard it is for you to drive by, fighting your instinct to slow down and crane your neck, trying to catch a glimpse of the wreckage?

We all have the same urge. Obviously, our response is related partially to a safety issue. It is smart and appropriate to slow down when you come upon a fresh accident that has not been pulled over to the side of the road. But, this is not the situation I am referring to here. I am talking about drivers in cars four lanes over, who are no longer in the path of the accident, that HAVE to slow to a crawl to gawk at the spectacle. It is just crazy!

The traffic problems caused by this phenomenon are so pervasive that a Federal "think tank" was commissioned to figure out why people do it. I could have saved them some time and money. People MUST gawk at accidents because of both Fundamental Seven and Fundamental Nine (our "intensity addiction" discussed later). The daily dose of intensity that viewing wrecks gives us is easy to explain. Less understood, though, is how Fundamental Seven and the "pointing finger" contributes to our need to gawk at accidents. Because we all have a bunch of psychological aspects that we work hard to hide, we therefore have a whole BUNCH of unconscious emotions "simmering" within our unconscious mind. The internal pressure created by these simmering aspects makes our pointing fingers pop out with intensity during crisis situations. Wrecks on the side of the road or police cars with their lights flashing are the perfect projection screens onto which our unconscious minds can throw or "project" all of our "bad" stuff that is simply too much for us to handle consciously. I know I am getting all deep on you here, but bear with me.

Let me say this another way: We stare, transfixed by the accident, and drive five miles an hour to gawk and get a "fix" from the crisis. The crisis gives our conscious mind a chance to point our finger at REALLY BAD STUFF. The more grisly the carnage, the better. We use crisis situations, even as small as fender benders, to project our BAD stuff outward, as if to say, "THERE! Over THERE! Look at that crunched heap of bad stuff over there!" Your mind shouts, "See, the badness is

NOT inside ME, it's over THERE!" Since we spend so much effort ignoring painful or uncomfortable thoughts and feelings, the external car crash or dramatic event acts as a symbol of the internal "crashes" we've had or experienced in our lives.

It is literally a relief for our conscious mind to pretend even for a moment that the really BAD stuff is outside of us, over on the side of the road. Remember, as I said earlier, we may not be **conscious** of the pressure created by our simmering unconscious aspects, but we can feel **something** bubbling inside of us. Crisis situations to which we have no personal attachments, such as wrecks or crimes sensationalized on T.V., are wonderful external events onto which we can easily project our own internal dramas. Therefore, they often *mesmerize* us momentarily. We are mystically transfixed by any outward event that is sufficiently equivalent to our own internal, psychological "train wrecks."

On a lighter note, the finger-pointing phenomenon is also a reason for the popularity of tabloid newspapers. If we can turn the focus from our personal dramas to the ones splashed across the pages of tabloids, we can enjoy a moment of peace from our own repressed "bad" stuff. Even highly conscious people seem to enjoy taking a "tabloid time out." I have many friends who secretly buy them in grocery store checkout lines and read them in "private," away from the judging eyes of their peers (who probably secretly buy them too). Friends laugh as they describe the elaborate, clandestine techniques they use to get the tabloid from the magazine rack, into their grocery cart and then into a grocery bag without anyone seeing it. These undercover fans say they know the stories these rags contain are mostly lies, but they cannot seem to stop themselves from buying them, anymore than drivers could pass by an accident without slowing down to gawk.

On a more serious note, I believe Fundamental Seven is also responsible for the quality of news (or the lack thereof) that we see on television, which largely highlights violent and/or sensational stories. These stories are also a convenient "screen" on which we can project our internal negative aspects. One station actually tried a "good news" channel. It bombed. Why? Don't people like good news? They do, but only in small doses, and usually only if it directly impacts something in **their** life. The good news of others makes many people feel jealous (see Fundamental Two). BAD news, on the other hand, makes many people feel less alone with their own stuff and relieved that the really bad stuff is not happening to them. Therefore it grabs the attention of most people.

In conclusion, what we ultimately learn from Fundamental Seven is that disowned, unacknowledged aspects of ourselves, aspects virtually invisible to us, are greatly influencing our thoughts, actions, and judgments toward others. That might initially be a disturbing realization. But, ultimately, there is good news. If we pay attention, our pointing fingers can act as "Geiger counters", giving us clues to the unconscious issues that lie deep within our psyches. Once we uncover those buried influences, they begin to lose their power, taking us another step closer to authentic living.

We all have multiple personalities.

> Behaviors you might see from OPs include markedly dif-
> ferent ways of behaving, feeling, and interacting when
> in different kinds of social or professional settings. These
> characteristics can range from flamboyant extroversion to
> quiet introversion, and can include behavioral mannerisms,
> speech patterns, language phrases, and voice tones and
> ranges.

Have you ever watched people when they are around babies? Have
you noticed how they talk to and interact with little ones when they are
trying to play with them or get their attention? Have you ever watched
that same baby-talking person when they are interacting with their
boss in a meeting, or someone they are attracted to, or with their parents? If you have had the chance to observe the same person in each
of these settings, you may have noticed that a lot of things change
about them from situation to situation. Their voice structure and tone,
postures, hand gestures and facial expressions may change. They may
even speak in very different vocabularies, including business-speak,
and family-speak including baby talk. If you listen closely and watch
carefully, you might be surprised by how dramatic these changes in
language and behavior can be from one situation to another.

Have you ever been driving for a long stretch of time and found yourself at one point "waking up" from a sort of hypnotic state? Did you notice that you covered a long stretch of road and that time had passed, but you couldn't remember how you got to where you are now? You are still on the road. You are safe and sound. You didn't really fall asleep. But there seems to be a gap in your memory from where you remember being to where you are now. Have you ever wondered who was driving during that time? Obviously, it was you… but, then again, it wasn't you because "you" just "woke up." The part of you that just came back to consciousness cannot remember anything about the missing time period and the missing stretch of road.

Have you ever felt thrown off track or awkward when someone you are socially close to unexpectedly stopped by while you were at work? Did you feel strangely stiff around this old friend or acquaintance? When you come home from work, does it take some time for you to "feel relaxed" or "in the mood" to greet and interact with your family and spouse? Does it seem as if one of your selves goes to work, and an entirely different one relates to your family when you get home? Have you ever taken someone home with you to visit your family of origin and had them comment about "how different you are" around your parents and family? Did they seem thrown off because they had never seen you act that way before?

If you answered "yes" to any of these questions, take heart! You have experienced the basic premise of Fundamental Eight in action. These examples illustrate the different "personalities" each of us adopts to cope with a wide variety of environments we encounter on a day-to-day basis. Throughout our lives, we develop different personalities that we feel are suitable for different situations. We even have common phrases to describe these different personalities. For example, do you have a "game face?" What does getting into "work mode" mean? The military trains men to "stay frosty" in tense situations. Who is that "evil twin" that many people joke about having within them?

Some of our personalities are trained into us by organizations, such as the military and corporations. But many reside naturally and unconsciously in us and simply pop out in certain situations before we even realize it. We all unknowingly have many different personalities—some pleasant, some not so pleasant, some advanced and wise, some regressed and immature.

When most people in my generation think of multiple personalities, they think of the movie *Sybil*. The main character had many different, distinct personalities that would "take over" depending on the emotional and physical environment she was in at the time. Many of us remember the speech idiosyncrasies and the dramatic changes in voice and body movements Sybil went through, depending on which personality was present. Her personalities even had different names to identify themselves. While the average person's behaviors and mannerisms do not change as dramatically as portrayed in the movie, I am suggesting that we all change our personalities depending on the situation. Usually those changes are much subtler than Sybil's. Sometimes they are not.

I first noticed this dynamic when I was hanging out one evening in a restaurant with a group of male friends. We were engaging in our usual bantering and joking around—typical "boys will be boys" behavior—when a beautiful woman walked by our table. Everyone's personality changed immediately. Some guys got quieter. Some got louder. Some became seductive. Some became protective. Some regressed to preverbal children, and others acted like rejected adolescents, cursing the interruption and the woman who caused it. One event that changed the environment—the presence of a woman—evoked many different personalities from the group, creating a whole new energy that a few minutes earlier was a homogeneous, male bonding experience.

Let's analyze what happened here. As the environment was changed by the presence of the woman, each man adopted the personality most capable of handling his specific, immediate needs and desires that were brought up by the new situation. Those whose primary reaction was sexual exhibited a "seducer personality" or an "attention-getter personality." Others who took on more of a "boy's club personality," felt irritated by her presence and the interruption it caused, and became mildly hostile. Still others felt the need to protect the woman (after all, we all knew each other's "evil twin" very well) and their "protective father" personality showed up. Within seconds, each man was expressing a very different personality—one that was not present moments earlier before the woman entered the room. After the woman left the room, POOF, we were all back into our "male bonding" personalities. Talk about multiple personalities! We were all Sybils!

As I have illustrated above, we all seem to have many different personalities within us that pop out when we need them the most, when we are frightened or excited, or when we are just plain exhausted. This ability to switch from one dominant personality to another depending on the situation has both positive and negative effects. On the negative side, there are terrifying reports of adults who have found themselves in a burning room, rushed to the door to escape, and were trapped because they could not remember how to work a doorknob. In their fear, they regressed to a much younger personality that did not know how to open a door. On the positive side, we hear of people who, in dangerous situations, act heroically in ways they would never have been capable of in their "normal" lives.

Most modern psychological thought suggests that there is one "Self" that is our truest nature, and that, throughout life, we each strive to become this healthy, actualized Self. Stated another way, the theory says that if we work hard enough to improve ourselves, we will become our "truest self" and everything will be fine and we will all live happily ever after.

I no longer believe that theory. While it might be arguable that our deepest, truest nature is a unified one of love and harmony, experience has shown me that we have many different personalities that can manifest these qualities in their own unique ways. I have come to believe that these coexisting different personalities inside of us make up the "Self." One person can have several loving personalities as well as several that are just simply mean as hell. I believe that the "Self" is simply a manifestation of **all** of our many personalities that show up in different situations.

In my experience, these personalities within us are very different from simple "moods". In fact, each of the personalities can display a broad range of moods. For example, a "protective parent" personality can be gentle, angry or firm, and still maintain its "protective parent" persona. Moods are smaller and more limited in behavioral range than personalities. Mood is to personality as weather is to climate. A tropical climate can have a cold front (weather) without changing its status as a tropical climate, just as the playboy/seducer can have a sad/angry mood and a flirty mood without the personality and behavior of that particular personality dissolving. Moods, then, add flavor to a personality.

The obvious next question is: "So, if this is the case, who is inside of me? How many personalities do I have inside this psyche of mine?" If I had to come up with a number offhand for how many different personalities we each have within us, I would have to guess that it is probably around ten for most people. These ten or so distinct personalities run portions or areas of our lives and often act independently of the other personalities. The "work" personality does its job at work and then, hopefully, the "family", "spouse", or "lover" personality takes over when we get home. It is not that the "work" and "home" personalities aren't similar in some ways; they can be and usually are. For example, they both could be very reserved, calm and quiet. But usually there are distinctly different qualities to each personality that shows up in different environments.

This can lead us to yet another question. Could some people have the same personality in two very different environments? Could the job personality be present in bed with a lover? Well, yes. Depending on a person's specific job personality, it could be very boring, but yes. Are there people out there who are boring and crabby at work **and** fun and loving in bed? Yes. There are as many different variations to this Fundamental as there are people. Each of us lives our life in our own distinct way. This theory does not predict the actual number of or characteristics of all the unique personalities that exist in people's psyches. At its most basic level, Fundamental Eight simply says we truly do act with very unique personalities and mannerisms in the variety of environments and situations we encounter. Understanding our unique personalities gives us a better handle on how we are behaving. This awareness can allow us to change our behaviors if they are not helpful to us.

One personal encounter that I will share with you dramatically pointed out to me the differences between a "work" personality and a "social" personality. My wife is a physician, and one day I went to meet her at her office at the end of her workday after her last surgery case. This is not something I do often. The front desk person told my wife I was waiting in her office. Excited to see me, she decided to stop by her office to say "hi" before changing out of her surgical scrubs. I was thumbing through a magazine while I waited. Suddenly, she jumped into her open office doorway in a playful kind of "gotcha" pose. As I looked up, I saw a mask-covered figure in "scrubs" jumping into the doorway, arms open as if for a hug, eyes beaming with excitement.

What followed this playful act was very strange, and we have continued to laugh about it for years. When our eyes met, we froze. Even though we were both excited to see each other, we just stared at each other, motionless. This was not a doctor/patient meeting, which she routinely engages in throughout the day. It was a doctor/husband meeting. She had not made the "switch" to wife mode yet. And I didn't know how to react to her. Her actions and my presence in her office were out of our usual context, and we both froze.

In the awkwardness of the moment, my wife flipped into "office autopilot." She dropped her hands to her sides, said, "I'll be finished in about twenty minutes," and turned and walked off. She went from "excited greeting" to business mode in a split second. She said later that she was very excited that I was there, but when she saw me in the office-setting while she was still in doctor mode, she was speechless. All she could think of to say was, "I'll be finished in twenty minutes." Our awkwardness was tangible. I felt it across the space between us. The experience was somewhat surreal.

Although I fully recognized her, in that moment our roles were incongruent. I was in my "husband" personality, and, because we were in her office, she was in her "doctor" (not wife) personality, and not in her "wife" personality. We could not connect the mutual playfulness and excitement we each felt in the moment to these totally different, extremely contrasting personalities. Talk about an odd couple! We were both excited to meet at the office, but the doctor and the lover did not mix in that setting AT ALL!

Thinking back on the situation, the awkwardness was not really related to the fact that she was wearing her work scrubs. She wears them home on occasion, and we sometimes curl up together or hug for long periods while she is still wearing them. The inability to connect was caused by the fact that she truly was in "doctor" personality, and that personality did not mix with my husband/lover personality. In that particular circumstance, it was as if she was a total stranger to me!

At this point you may be thinking, "Well, all this is very interesting, but what is the advantage of believing the theory of Fundamental Eight rather than saying we have different moods in different environments?" The huge advantage relates to the individual talents and resources that are available to us as we experience and express different personalities. Several years ago when I was first toying with this theory, I ran it by a colleague of mine. Her response was, "Shouldn't we all be integrating one self throughout the different areas of our lives? Wouldn't that be more consistent and valuable?" The question intrigued me. It certainly seemed reasonable to want a consistent, single "self" that we could rely on and apply across different situations throughout our lives.

Then one night while I was facilitating a group therapy session, I made one illuminating comment that intrigued several group members. You know, it was one of those ten or twelve really wise things we might say in a lifetime. I realized in that moment that I could not have accessed that wisdom in any state other than the "therapist" personality I "take on" in sessions. My "social, fun loving" personality would never have said something of that caliber. My "crazy friend" personality or my "lover" personality would never come up with something that profound. Here is another example on the next page:

"I remember this one session and I'm there just totally immersed in the session and my client is so deep and you can tell she is on the verge of a breakthrough, you can just tell. She has just recounted this long string of events she has been through the past year and trying to string them all together in some linear way and I am just going with it and she says to me, almost playfully, 'Why did all these things happen to me...what does it all mean?'

And I think in that split second, 'Oh my God, she is just so ready to hear something significant out of me and I have no idea how to answer it in an any meaningful way that could put all of the events together,' and BAM without missing a beat, not one, my mouth opens up and says:

'The reason you broke up with him is because he represents an old relationship pattern that you have carried most of your life and you are just now ready to open to a new way of relating to the world and others. You left him because your eyes are different now and your heart surgery three weeks later conforms with the interior heart opening you've had either as a result of the change within you or at least is symbolic of it. You are seeing with your new eyes. The car accident the day before you broke up was the psyche's way of telling you the old ways of fourteen years, the same age as your car, were over. That is why it was totaled and you had to buy a new one to start your "new" phase of life. Your friends now seem not to be such good friends—you said they had all seemed to change—because now that you are seeing from a more open heart space you have lifted a veil that previously made them appear nice when in fact they were **always** jealous and competitive with you. You just see the real truth now. And now that you see this, you feel isolated and totally alone...not because you broke up with your boyfriend and are somehow being punished for making the wrong decision, but because you are just now seeing clearly the isolation you have been truly experiencing **in** the relationship for several years. You woke up with different eyes to see that your world for many years has been an illusion you did not want to see until your psyche felt it was capable of handling the resultant isolation and aloneness. Now you can enter a whole new world and let go of another layer of illusion that no longer serves you.'

And I said all this to her without even taking a breath. Before I opened my mouth I had no idea how to put together everything that was happening in her life let alone what it all meant. And, Wham, there it was, pouring out of my mouth like some planned monologue. That wasn't my knowledge, I'll tell you that. Even **I** was impressed by the information, and it was supposed to be coming from **me**.

From actual conversation

This experience and this example solidified my theory that what makes these sides of us "personalities" (and not merely "roles" or "moods") is the specific, different and distinct resources they each have available to them. Roles are simply behaviors that someone plays out that can easily be witnessed by others. Moods are simply emotional temperament. Personalities, on the other hand, carry with them unique resources that become accessible only when we are in those specific personalities. Not much wisdom is accessible to me when I am in my "fun-loving" personality. And I am not that much fun to be around when I am in my "therapist" personality (sad as that may be). I probably could not arouse many women in "therapist" mode, nor could I pass on much insight in "lover" mode. Once we go "into" a specific personality, we gain access to the distinct talents and resources specific to that personality. It is as if every personality has its own unique "tool belt" of gifts and talents.

Because I have observed and experienced the broader base of skills and resources available to us through the variety of distinct personalities we each have, I finally concluded that I disagree with my colleague's position that it is best to have only one, true personality. I believe that a person with one primary personality would not have access to the broader range of resources available to several personalities. My basic theory, unfortunately, would be hard to prove because, to do so, we would need "control" subjects. And I do not believe there is anyone living who actually has only one integrated personality, no matter what they think or believe about themselves. I believe we **all** have multiple personalities that give us access to a wider range of talents and resources than any one personality could possibly offer.

I'd like to throw in a small word here about opposites and spectrums of personality. I believe that once we are "in" one personality, its opposite is also present, lying deep within us. Here is an example of a person who has two very distinct, opposite sides. For discussion's sake, I will use a rather extreme example of a killer because the opposites of the spectrum are more easily seen. Most people engage in less extreme opposite behaviors and are therefore more difficult to use for illustration purposes.

In the movie *Casino*, which is based on a true story, Joe Pesci plays a real life character who is a psychotic killer. This same brutal murderer never missed making his son's breakfast. Never mind that he might have a freshly murdered body in his trunk and be on his way to the dump to make a "drop". He would stop whatever he was doing at the same time each morning, clean himself up and fix his son's breakfast. How do we reconcile the presence of the "psychotic killer" and the "nurturing father" in the same person when they are obviously opposite ends of the spectrum?

The answer is...balance. Our psyche, like the physical world, is always trying to come into balance. For every negative personality that lives in your psyche, you will also have a personality that is its positive counterbalance. This is not to say that every negative *behavior* a person displays is physically counterbalanced by a positive behavior. Some people behave negatively most of the time. But, simply stated, our psyche strives to reach and maintain balance over time. You have within you the positive personality traits that will balance your negative personality traits. This does not necessarily mean you will ever display these positive traits (or negative traits) to anyone. But they are there, waiting for you to access them. Most people never achieve full psychological balance, but the opposite personalities needed to reach that balance are present, willing and able to be used, if you choose to access them.

"Killers," and by this I mean actual murderers, always seem to have a tender side that appears in certain specific settings. They can become overly emotional when they listen to music or observe someone harming pets. They may tear up when they see or hear a newborn baby cry. You can see these opposites in action when you listen to interviews with neighbors of convicted serial killers. They often describe the psychotic killer as "quiet, sweet, and nice."

On the other side of the coin, soft, gentle personalities carry a ruthless, violent opposite that may not appear often—but is rarely forgotten when it does. Anyone who has crossed their favorite loving teacher or adult may have felt the contrasting sting of stern disapproval from them and been shocked at its severity.

Let me give you another, more common, example of how these opposites in people show themselves.

"My daughter is three years old, now understand that before we start okay? We are in this beautiful park on a great day and everything is gorgeous and the grass is so green and the trees are so colorful. I think it is her first visit to a park.

She points to a pile of trash someone left behind over in the corner by a bench and she says, 'Mommy what is that over there?'

I see what she is pointing at and say kind of casually, 'Oh, that is just some trash someone left behind.'

She looks away and takes this loooong pause. 'Mommy,' she says in this disapproving tone, 'the Earth doesn't liiiiiiike thaaaaat.'

Can you believe it? She is only three and she sounds like some 80 year old, wise person.

From actual conversation

Have you ever proudly repeated to a friend something unbelievably wise that was said by one of your children? Following my theory about opposites, when a child is born, though he is innocent and inexperienced in the world, a "wise elder" personality is also present within this child. This wise elder may not express himself in words for a few years, or, for that matter, do much talking at all. He is present nonethless. I believe that when children occasionally come up with profound pieces of wisdom, they are simply accessing their "elder" personalities.

In my experience, personality opposites are expressed in a variety of ways. Sometimes they are played out during different phases in a person's life. For example, a person may express a rough, volatile nature during the first twenty years of their life, followed by a twenty-year sensitive, caring phase. One of the more commonly seen examples of this shifting to opposites is the Drugs to Christianity shift. You know, the drug addict wild man who later in life turns to Religion and becomes the most avid church promoter. Also, recently we have had public examples of Fundamentalist Christian leaders caught in drug scandals. It goes both ways.

Sometimes the opposites are present throughout the course of a person's life, but show up in different arenas such as work vs. home or private life vs. social life. Sometimes, and this gets **really** complicated, a person will choose to be in relationship with a person whose personality is entirely opposite from theirs in an attempt to achieve balance within the context of the relationship. In this case, each individual "acts out" behaviors opposite to those of the dominant personality of the other person, but the relationship as a whole carries an overall balance. See how complex this all gets?

To recap what we have gone over in this Fundamental, we all have multiple personalities, and each positive personality has a corresponding negative personality. Opposite personalities can be expressed in different life phases and/or in different life arenas. Ultimately, everything in the world, including the personalities that live in our psyches, strives for balance. As I mentioned before, rarely is complete balance achieved, but moving toward that goal is a worthy pursuit.

If you are still with me on all this opposite spectrum and balance stuff, you probably have twenty questions circling around inside your head. They are probably being shouted out by various personalities that like or dislike the idea of being "found out" and explored. With a little bit of attention to the opposing thoughts you are thinking, you can see (or hear) that this phenomenon is quite complex. (Remember, this book is meant to evoke discussions!)

If you want to hone in on the basic premise of this principle, here is what you can try in the real world: The next time someone says you are not acting like yourself, simply ask them, "Which self are you talking about?"

So, take heart, you corporate climbing, conservative pinstripe wearing weekend adventurers. You are not crazy or a Sybil. And you may not be simply relieving frustration built up during your workweek by yelling at football games, playing paintball or hiking. You are most likely playing out the drama of your opposing personalities moving toward wholeness and psychological balance.

We are all addicted to Intensity.

> Behaviors you might see from OPs include: highly dramatic, overblown emotional reactions to mundane events; acting out of the "drama queen or king" personality; constant gossiping about and/or involvement in a high number of crises—real or made up; substance and food addictions including abuse of caffeine, high energy drinks or exercise; repeated choice of abusive or neglecting partners in relationships.

The quick and easy way to sum up the majority of behaviors covered by this Fundamental is to say that Fundamental Nine rules the "Drama Queen or King" personality that lives in all of us. You probably know the most common manifestation of this personality all too well: the victimized soul that is always surrounded by crisis and constantly moans, "Oh, woe is me... what will I ever do about _____ (fill in the blank with any number of issues). How will I ever make it through this?" This cry (or should we say whine?) is usually punctuated with the tonal equivalent of the back of the hand being placed firmly against the forehead—a move that is often referred to as the 'victim's salute.'

"She was always that way, nothing that ever happened to her was usual. If it was an illness, she had to have the worst case ever. If her children got sick, she would take them to the Emergency room, I mean for having a runny nose. And then she would tell everyone every detail of the story. Beginning to end, reaching the conclusion that she thought the doctor under-diagnosed their sickness. Everything in her life had to be a catastrophe. It got to be a bore."

From actual conversation

We all know this type of person. And I would wager we all have engaged in some version of this behavior at some time in our lives. If you doubt this, think back to that woeful time when your first teenage relationship ended. Or, if you were a late bloomer, take yourself back to the first time you shared a real crisis with a college friend. Remember how dire the situation was at the time and how HORRIBLE it seemed? You and your friend most likely talked about this devastating situation non-stop for days, reliving every minute detail over and over.

Now, come forward in time. Think about a situation when a family member did something "unforgivable" to you, and you were once again "devastated." If nothing along these lines pops into your head, recall a recent conversation with a friend who bored you for hours with their long list of complaints about the "outrageous" behavior of one of their neighbors...or their spouse. If none of these situations was truly a "life and death" scenario, you were both probably caught up in the middle of a HIGH DRAMA!

Every workplace has at least one of these people in their workforce. They come in on Mondays and spout forth every detail about the most recent crisis in their relationship or family and how desperate they are and how horrible this event either is or will be if they don't do something quickly. Outside of work, they are the friends who have constant, critical, financial and/or relationship problems and talk incessantly about them. They repeatedly choose abusive partners to be in relationship with, or, no matter how bad it gets, never leave their present abusive partner. But they will complain incessantly about them. They are also the people who are, or become, substance abusers.

All of these people, in their own ways, are addicted to intensity. True, we all have problems from time to time, and we naturally talk about them when we are in the throes of dealing with them. However, intensity addicts are different from persons who occasionally share their problems with friends or co-workers. The difference between the two can be identified by the intensity of their descriptions and the frequency of their crises.

When people who are not addicted to intensity (let's call them solution-focused) share an issue with a friend, it is not described as "the end of the world" or "life and death." Solution-focused people are usually not sobbing uncontrollably while they describe the situation. Instead, they recount the circumstances of the issue, share their concern, ask for advice or some empathy, and move on.

When an intensity addict describes a situation, it is **always** a MAJOR crisis. The intensity addict exaggerates events beyond the severity level of the actual circumstances. Every nuance is described with hand-ringing drama and/or is punctuated by the "victim's salute."

Frequency of crisis, the second telltale characteristic of an intensity addict, is often easier to recognize. Intensity addicts are **constantly** in crisis. And, if they lack a new crisis to complain about, they will rehash the tale of a recently passed one. I am not saying that solution-focused people do not have crises from time to time. They do. But, while the intensity addict is always in crisis mode, for solution-focused people, true crises are rare. If you are constantly helping someone through one crisis after another, they are probably addicted to intensity.

Having read this initial description, many parents out there are probably saying to themselves, "Hey! This sounds exactly like my teenager!" They are right! Teenagers live in a world of emotional intensity.

They thrive on it. And, yes, they are addicted to it. Every event in a teenager's life is MAJOR to them. If you are ever around teenagers, watch how animatedly they discuss very mundane events.

"Joe is going out with Beth next Saturday!" says Teen One.

"NOOOO WAAAAAYYYY! NOOOO WAAY!" replies Teen Two.

"I caaaannnn't believe it…..I'll just die….I'll just die!" says Teen One, with her hand pressed to her forehead and tears beginning to fall.

And so on and so on. This is life in the teen world. What someone is wearing, what someone said to someone else, who is going out with whom, who might break up with whom—everything is front-page headline news, better known as a "crisis." Although a teenage intensity addiction may be hard to live with, there is good news behind this rain cloud! Just hang in there! This may not be a long-term problem. Intensity addiction is age and phase appropriate for teenagers. Many will (hopefully) grow out of it!

But now, the bad news. Some adults **never** grow out of this phase. Instead, they thrive throughout their lives on the attention they receive when they are in the middle of a crisis. The payoffs they get are just too tasty to give up.

So why is addiction to intensity a problem? You can probably think of several normal, productive people who constantly exaggerate their situations and make mountains out of molehills. What is the harm of this? To answer this question we need to understand why people maintain intensity addictions in the first place. I purposefully left this Fundamental for last because having an understanding of Fundamental Six (The Immature Masculine always runs from or tries to dominate the Feminine) helps us to understand what lies beneath Fundamental Nine, and why this is problematic.

Put very simply, people who are addicted to intensity attempt to flood themselves with *superficial* intensity, rather than feel the *genuine*, deep emotions connected to a situation. They avoid their true feelings, by burying them under the intensity created by an emotional drama or an activity that promotes an intense feeling. Thrill seeking is another form of intensity addiction as well as something as simple as an intense exercise regimen. The goal here is: ANYTHING that is INTENSE that causes a rush of endorphins!

The intensity-addicted life contains a paradox. Intensity addicts manufacture intense emotion to **avoid** intense emotion. Isn't that strange? Read that again. They manufacture intense emotions in an attempt to avoid intense emotions. Why would someone go to all that trouble? It is because the emotions they manufacture are just that—manufactured. Because they are artificial and shallow, they have a less powerful impact than genuine emotions. I believe the reason there are so many intensity addicts in our culture is because we are generally so terrified of our deeper, more heartfelt emotions, that we will avoid feeling them at all costs.

As a side bar, I also believe this avoidance of deeper emotions is the underlying cause of commitment phobias. I bet you will know at least one eligible bachelor or bachelorette who says he or she wants to settle down, but who just cannot seem to commit to a serious relationship. In my experience, they are too afraid of the depth of feeling a serious relationship might thrust upon them. To avoid that depth of feeling, they stay in a series of short-term relationships that do not deepen emotionally. Instead, they constantly create a never-ending cycle of break-up crises.

Now, let's look a little more closely at the dynamics played out by a drama queen/king intensity addict so that we can come to a better understanding of how people use manufactured emotions to avoid deeper emotions. A good starting point is to examine the dynamics of a much more easily recognizable addict: a drug addict.

A drug addict uses drugs to avoid painful feeling states. Rather than feel sadness or grief, they get "high" (intensity). Rather than feel loneliness or fear, they get "high" (intensity). Ironically, over time, the drug addiction itself usually causes even more painful feeling states surrounding loss of job, loss of loved ones, and loss of Self. This causes the addict to expand the use of their substance (or intensity-of-choice) to avoid the deeper, more agonizing emotions.

This use of "highs" to avoid (depth) "lows" can also be seen in people ruled by Fundamental Six. Intensity addiction is also a technique often used by the Immature Masculine to avoid and/or dominate the Feminine. (Sound familiar?) Remember, intensity addicts are so fearful of feeling genuine, deep emotions (Feminine), that they use the intensity of superficial crises to block out emotions by overriding them with excitement. The same is true of the Immature Masculine in a person. If the Immature Masculine can stay EXCITED (a superficial state), like the intensity addict, neither of them has to feel any genuine depth of any emotion.

Let's turn back now to the Intensity Addict's emotional life. As mentioned before, this repeated process of emotional avoidance creates even bigger problems because it negatively impacts all of the Intensity Addict's relationships. When someone runs from their emotions long enough, their fear of those emotions grows. They have to find a way to avoid connections and situations that put them into an emotionally vulnerable state. Because of this, the Intensity Addict ultimately becomes isolated and feels alone in the world, even when surrounded by people. From the outside looking in, people generally experience Intensity Addicts as distant, superficial, and ultimately, unreachable. People describe their experience of being in relationship with an intensity addict by saying they could never figure out how to get to know them or feel close to them.

You might be asking at this point, how does the Intensity Addict's emotional avoidance process relate to, say, my friend Sally at work who is in constant crisis?"

Sally's intensity addiction is still fueled by the same psychological and emotional desire—to avoid genuine, deep feelings. Sally's exaggerations and perpetual crises cause her to become increasingly isolated in several ways. First, remember she has to be around "crisis" to avoid her deeper feelings. This means Sally is emotionally immature and generally "superficial." Because of this, she cannot maintain a relationship with anyone who is comfortable with having and expressing deep emotions. Guess which type of men she will allow into her life— equally superficial, immature men who are emotionally unexpressive. Because emotionally immature men often have poor impulse control, they also have a higher probability of becoming physical abusers.

Coincidental, isn't it? Sally, who thrives on crisis, actually is only attracted to the types of men who would naturally bring crisis and intensity to the relationship table. While she might not be in relationship with a physical abuser, she will certainly attract someone who, like her, is uncomfortable with emotion and is, therefore, unable to express it. In this case, guess what Sally's biggest complaint will probably be? You guessed it…how unaffectionate and distant her partner is. Intensity addicts often attract emotionally distant—if not physically abusive—partners who will provide them with continuous relationship crises.

Poor Sally has yet another problem. People get tired of hearing about her ongoing crises. Over time, they begin to avoid her. The only people willing to be Sally's friends are other intensity addicts who thrive on Sally's problems. And Sally thrives on theirs. Even though Sally and these friends may appear to be bonded, eventually Sally may fall victim to yet another kind of isolation. Why would Sally be rejected by her own kind? Well, even intensity addicts have an acceptable range of intensity tolerance.

Although all intensity addicts by definition thrive on intensity— there are different kinds—some prefer less while others prefer more. Even among drug users there are acceptable and unacceptable intensities. For some, alcohol abuse is fine, but cocaine use is not. For others, cocaine use is fine, but heroin use is not. Every addict has an intensity range they will tolerate. And they also approve of certain ways of getting their "fixes," whether their fix is related to an event, a behavior, a relationship, or a specific substance. How does this affect Sally? People who have only a mild need for intensity, and those who do not get their fix from the relationship arena, will often find Sally's crises just "too much" to be around. This leads to another level of social isolation for Sally.

Some people feed their intensity addiction in ways that are not only socially acceptable but are actually thriving cultural trends. A few extra cups of coffee each day may give someone their fix. These caffeine lovers may not be in emotional crisis every week, but BEWARE— they may take you out if you stand between them and the coffee machine in the morning! You wonder why there seems to be a Starbucks on every corner these days? Could this be an ingenious marketing plan based on Fundamental Nine?

"And what about Jolt cola, did you hear about that—-twice the caffeine and twice the sugar. What the hell have we come to? It's never enough. Gotta get the rush and twice the punch is the only way. The only person I can imagine really wanting this stuff is the same guy who thinks Jerry Springer is a talk show. You know, unless there is wrestling onstage within five minutes of a guest appearance it's just too boring—-can't you just hear it…

'Hey honey, get me another Jolt cola, Jerry's about to start, oh, and bring me my cigarettes too will ya…and while you're at it, bring me that line of cocaine you talked me out of earlier.

From actual conversation

Some people use strict (often unhealthy) diets or intense exercise regimens to maintain their own personally acceptable level of intensity. And when all else fails, they can always slug down one of the numerous new "energy" drinks, which are guaranteed to give you a buzz. So, whether they use dramatic relationships, constant crises, exercise or something else, intensity junkies will do what they must do to feed their intensity addiction.

Let's get back to Sally for another minute. Believe it or not, Sally has yet another problem. If she is not surrounded by enough intensity to drown out her uncomfortable feelings, she will manufacture dramas of her own. She will either set up a crisis of her own making or stir up the pot of her family and friends to prod someone into blowing up.

Eureka! She has caused a side crisis in which she can become involved. If Sally is a parent, she may call up the child that is most easily agitated and just happen to mention the most charged issue between them. BOOM! Explosive fight ensues. Emotional intensity strikes again! Keep your ears open when someone calls you up out of the blue and picks a fight or jabs at you about a sensitive subject. You are most likely dealing with an intensity addict trying to get a "fix."

Let's focus on Sally's children for a minute. They, obviously, have grown up in a home filled with intensity. If children of intensity addicts grow out of their own teenage intensity addictions, they will often avoid one or both parents later in life because they realize that every time they are around them, the parent provokes them into a rage. The intensity addicted parent will immediately feed off the child's rage (the parent's first "fix"), and then tell the tale of their "horrible fight" to someone else later, getting a double "fix" from a single event. If repeated frequently over time, this behavior, as described before in relation to drug addiction, ends up causing emotional isolation and aloneness...even from the intensity addict's own children.

Fundamental Nine also explains the popularity of such shows as *Jerry Springer*, *WWF Wrestling*, *Fear Factor*, and *Survivor*. These shows vicariously feed people's need for intensity. Intellectual discussions are boring to an intensity addict, but throw in a Jerry Springer "cheatin' trailer trash" episode or a good wrestling face-off and you have a full hour of emotional anesthesia. A good intensity addict really doesn't care that much about how the Survivors excel in their physical contests; they get their thrill by watching emotionally intense backstabbing, manipulation, or dramatic failures. Remember, the objective here is to flood the senses with intensity of any kind to anesthetize all other feelings.

Television producers have, perhaps unknowingly, used the principles of Fundamental Nine for years. It does not matter if it is verbal wrestling on a talk show, manipulative backstabbing on a deserted island, eating live tarantulas and bugs, or the twisted plots of soap operas. The winning formula is to make whatever happens on the show INTENSE!

Here is another example from the media world. Remember when standing ovations for a performer or a performance were rare and moving? Not anymore. In today's programmed world, every time a talk show host walks onto the stage, the audience is on their feet. Even a brand new host that has not yet become a household name can expect this greeting. Why? Because audiences are worked into a frenzy by pre-show entertainment, which makes the show intense even before it starts! In high-intensity television, every entrance merits a standing ovation, and every show is an Extravaganza! Just tune into *Jerry Springer* and you can see how producers keep the intensity boiling, season after season!

If you are still not sure how intensity and excitement mask true feelings, go to an amusement park when you are feeling neutral or down and take a roller coaster ride. Try to stay depressed during the actual ride. You can't do it! The flood of intensity while riding is too great. When the ride is over, after a period, you might begin to feel depressed or low again. If you are an intensity junkie, you will start to look for ways to get another intensity fix. One quick and easy solution? Hop back on the roller coaster, ride it again, and repeat as necessary. After a while, the roller coaster will begin to loose its thrill. But, have no fear. There is a whole park out there filled with all sorts of rides!

This is exactly how intensity addicts use crises throughout their lives. They "ride" each crisis as many times as they can, until it looses its thrill. If one situation is not enough to anesthetize them after a while, they will mysteriously find themselves in another crisis, and then another …and another…until it **is** enough.

Other than substance abuse, relationships are the most prevalent arena in which people play out their intensity addictions. Why choose a partner that is stable, loyal and giving (read: boring) when you can choose an untrustworthy, unreliable and erratic partner— the intensity addict's **dream** catch. There is never a boring minute with that kind of partner. Show me a person who chooses only unreliable, cheating, distant partners, and I will show you an intensity addict. "Why do I choose such horrible mates?" I am often asked. I answer, "Because the loyal, reliable, giving ones are too boring for you."

Many people have also asked me why the really "bad" boys and girls always seem to get the most sexual attention from the opposite sex. The answer, I believe, is that we live in a society of intensity addicts. Reliable, loyal mates do not create enough crises to stimulate an intensity addict. But "bad" boys and girls do.

I believe intensity addiction is also the reason that "black sheep" (troublemakers) in families are often secretly the favorite of their parents. There is a wonderful scene in the movie *Legends of the Fall* that captures this point. The movie tells the story of a family living in the west during the early 1900's. The focus of the movie is the rivalry between two brothers—a "good" one who follows all the rules and a "bad" one who does not. At the very end of the film, the "good" brother says to the "bad" brother, "I have spent my entire life doing the right thing and following all the rules. You have done nothing but break all the rules and cause hurt to others, and it is you who everyone loves the most."

Why do nice guys fade from our hearts and memories more quickly than rebels? I believe it is because intensity gets noticed. It pushes our buttons and elicits emotion from us. Intensity is memorable and, to a point, attractive. And it makes us, if only for a moment, feel fully alive.

Before summarizing all of the territory we have covered in this Fundamental, it's important to note that the whole process of creating or involving ourselves in crisis after crisis is an unconscious one. When intensity addicts are "in" their addiction, they don't realize that they are doing anything problematic. They think **life** is throwing crisis after crisis at them…for the umpteenth time. Surely this is not their own doing! Most of us feel everyday "Life" throws plenty enough troubles in our path to keep us "juiced up" and to keep the everyday doldrums away. But, for the intensity addict, the normal dramas of life are not enough to distract them from the intensity of unfelt emotions that are building up inside of them.

In conclusion, I want to re-emphasize that intensity addiction is normal and developmentally appropriate during our teenage years.

(Besides, this allows me to get away with the sweeping generalization that we are all intensity addicts!) The important issue becomes whether or not we move out of this addiction as we get older. If we do not, we will pursue crisis after crisis to keep feeding a need for ever increasing stimulation. As a result, intensity addicts become more isolated, depressed and lonely, which feeds the circle of looking for more intensity to cover deep, fearful feelings. This need to constantly "up the emotional drama ante," as you can imagine, is dangerous to one's psychological health and can even become dangerous to one's physical well being. For this reason, I intensely recommend you avoid the path of excessive intensity.

ALMOST FINAL THOUGHTS

We have now been through the nine Fundamentals and, if you are still with me, congratulations! That means you are a person with a somewhat open, curious mind and that you may have wondered from time to time why people do some crazy or hurtful things. Or you may have scanned through the Fundamentals when you picked up this book and decided I was crazy. (This has been open to debate for quite some time!)

No matter what attracted you to this book, if you are reading this conclusion, you are just the person I had in mind when I wrote it. I began this book by saying I wanted to write something about human behavior that has not been covered often in other books and I have done this by talking about human behavior and motivation in a broader, more general context. As you read through each of these Fundamentals, did questions pop up for you about whether they apply to this situation or to that person or whether a particular statement is true at all?

GOOD! THEN I HAVE ACCOMPLISHED MY GOAL—
GENERATING THOUGHT, QUESTIONS AND DISCUSSION.

It is less important to me that you accept these Fundamentals as truth than that they provoke thought and discussion in your own mind. As I said earlier, this book is intended to **begin** a discussion. Where are these Fundamentals true for you and where are they not? Are you sure, and how do you really know? What would others say about **you**? Could these Fundamentals explain why we are sometimes caught in behavior patterns that don't make logical sense? What other more global issues might they address and explain? Could they possibly explain psychological motivations that underlie the behaviors of entire nations?

All of these are valid questions worthy of discussion and thought, but the first most relevant and important step is to use these concepts to understand your Self and your behaviors at a deeper level. By asking yourself how these Fundamentals pertain to you and the people that you relate to each day, you can discover where the true gold of these Fundamentals lies.

If I were writing this book in a popular self-help format, this would be the portion of the book where I would give you several exercises that would help you apply the Fundamentals to your own life. They would be intended to help you move beyond the patterns that keep you enslaved by the various behaviors described in the Fundamentals. I am not going to do that in this book. (The Masculine dominant readers out there just sighed in relief. The Feminine dominant readers just got disappointed.) Let me explain why I am not including exercises in this book.

The first, rather small reason is that I believe most people are really not interested in workbook exercises, even if they say they are. On top of that, I believe some people actually feel guilty when they do not complete them. I certainly do not want to evoke that response either.

Another reason is that I am not sure that these kinds of exercises actually help people get past their psychological issues. They might, but I am just not sure they do. I do not want to include a bunch of exercises and even remotely suggest that if you complete them, they will somehow cure you of your problems. How would you feel if you did them and nothing happened?

I also don't want the people who would **not** do the exercises to feel that they are lazy and uninterested, or even worse, that they failed to take advantage of a situation that would have "cured" them. Just look at all those bad feelings I have saved you from by not including exercises (take a look back at Fundamental 3: Genuine Interest in and Attention to Others...)! There is no point in creating a scenario that might invite failure, or that would support the illusion that by completing exercises your life will be miraculously transformed.

Now, although the reasons given above are important, let me tell you the one BIG reason I am not including an exercise portion in this book. It has to do with the philosophy of change I have put together after twenty-five years of experience as a therapist and a coach. In attempting to better understand my own unique style of coaching and therapy, I have asked myself many times over the years, "What is it that I do as a coach? What is it about my approach that uniquely helps people? What is the technique that makes me an effective agent of change for people?" The answer has changed many, many times in my mind. I used to think the gift I offered was insight. That thought later advanced to the belief that I offered "clever insight." Later I thought it was because I so deeply love what I do that it enhanced my impact on others. Recently though, I have come to a brand new belief that clarifies my real goal in continuing to do this work.

I believe now that my most important purpose—and challenge—is simply to get people **interested** in their issues. If all of the experience and skill that I have developed over the years simply gets you interested in an issue that is bothering you, I will have completed 50% of my job. Sounds weird, doesn't it? It appears oddly simple.

The truth is that getting people interested in their own issues is not easy at all. Most people do not care one whit about most of their psychological workings and would never think about them for one minute if some external problem didn't whack them upside the head. This "whack" might be a relationship, job-related, or emotional problem that just keeps getting in their way and will not leave them alone.

It might be an issue that literally nags at them through the voice of a spouse, a friend, or a boss. Or sometimes a thought or emotion keeps cropping up often enough to bother them. The vehicle that finally brings someone's attention to an issue does not matter. What matters is that it is gnawing at them so much, they are now motivated to do something to stop it!

This is often when people come to see somebody like me. They want me to "fix" their nagging problem—and QUICK! This impatience has created an entire industry that caters to a society that loves pills and takes tons of them (literally). Everyone wants the quick fix and the pharmaceutical companies are here to help! Take this pill and you can go about your business without missing a beat. In fact, take this pill for this and this pill for that, and then take this pill for the problem that pill is causing—and all your problems will disappear. Our airwaves are so filled with pill commercials that I am not even sure what the pills they are advertising actually do. I just know that if I take them I will soon be relaxing in a hammock or be able to throw a football through a tire swing. The point here is that most people are not interested in taking the time to work on themselves; they want a QUICK FIX. This impatience and the lack of interest in the personal process of change makes my job that much harder.

As bad as this sounds to my "Type A" readers, there are truly no quick fixes in the psychological arena. Psychological issues generally have a cause and effect component to them. And most people are not interested in what actually caused their problems. Notice that word again: "interested." It keeps coming up in my sentences, unfortunately preceded by the word: "not." After years of dealing with my clients' issues—and my own—I realized that if someone is going to effectively change themselves, they have to first be **interested**, and then solutions begin to spring from there.

So, those of you who are not yet willing to give another approach a chance may say, "What if I **am interested** in exercises? Would you give me some then?" Instead of answering that question, I would like to propose another: What if **interest** was all you needed to cure yourself of every problem you have? What if all you had to bring to the table to "attack your issues" is genuine interest in and attention to the issue at hand? What if this were the key to solving your problems over time? Would that change your mind about having to complete some questionably effective exercises to improve your situation? My bet is—yes. And since I am not going to give you any exercises anyway, let me give you instead a fuller explanation of this principle of change.

I believe that attention or interest is a genuinely magical force. Put simply, your attention to or interest in a thing changes that thing. Quantum physics has taught us that one cannot separate the observer from what is being observed. Placing our attention or interest on something brings change. So the solution to any problem, in my opinion, lies in the attention or interest we give to finding it.

You may be asking, "how does this magic work?" Well, here are my thoughts. Once you become genuinely interested in, say, how to become more courageous and less fearful in your life, things related to this area of your life can begin to change. You might, for example, notice that you become more aware of your thoughts and behaviors around courage and fear. You might realize that you are fearful in certain situations that you weren't aware of before.

For example, one day out of the blue as you reach for the radio button in your car, a thought like this may run through your head: "Huh, when I am in a silent car without the radio blasting, I am a little nervous and uncomfortable." Then because you notice this thought and are interested in **that** observation, you might wonder what would happen if you **didn't** have the radio blasting or, for that matter, playing at all. Then you might become interested in watching your emotions when there is silence in the car and you may follow those feelings to see where they led you. You might even jump from there (because you are now so darn interested) to wondering about other situations where you feel uncomfortable when there is silence. You may then remember that when you are in a social setting, silence is truly uncomfortable for you.

All of these observations came to mind simply because you got interested in the issue of fear and where and how it affects you in your life. In this somewhat roundabout way, the issue you are interested in can change directly **because** of your interest and attention. See what I mean? It is like magic! The expression "awareness cures" that is used in psychological circles comes from this phenomenon. It is not just an intellectual insight or thought that cures; it is the aspect of engaging the awareness of a conflict or issue over time that brings about the "cure."

So, because of the power of interest and attention, I believe my job is to find a creative way to get you **interested** in your own issue. From there, you can change yourself. And if this explanation is not enough, and by golly don't you think it ought to be, there is more! There is something even deeper supporting this principle that works below the conscious level and creates an even greater effect. Once again, in psychological circles, this is referred to as the theory of "psychic compensation." If that phrase seems intimidating, don't worry. I am going tell you a story that I was told to explain it.

During a seminar, a teacher I respect very much began talking about an obscure European movie he ran across that had tremendous impact on people who saw it. It was the horrific story of a woman caught alone by a band of convicts, who kidnapped her and did every terrible thing imaginable to her before she luckily escaped. When they discovered she was gone, they started chasing her. The movie followed her journey through treacherous geographical terrain as she tried to make her way back to safety, which, if my memory serves me, included a fiancé she was soon to marry. At the very end of the movie (sorry to ruin it for you) she is caught in quicksand and is slowly dragged down to her death. The last scene shows a close-up of her fist, which she holds defiantly above her head, until it too is dragged under. The End.

I can tell you this: after hearing this summary of the movie, no one in that room was rushing out to see it. Several people in the room audibly gasped as the teacher told the ending. Horrible sounding movie, eh?

So what does all this have to do with "psychic compensation?" Let's first assume someone could actually sit through the entire movie. For American audiences, this is unlikely. American moviegoers, for the most part, will not tolerate unhappy endings. But, for those who make it to the end, it has an interesting, though discomforting, effect: it leaves the viewer hanging with the protagonist's (the woman's) unresolved conflict—getting back to safety, her true love, and a wedding.

The person viewing the movie is left hanging with an intense psychological discomfort as they leave the theatre. Our heroine did not resolve the problem of escaping and returning to safety. An important reason that this movie, and others like it, are so disconcerting is that the psyche of the individual cannot tell the difference between so called "reality" and what is showing on a movie screen. Because of this, lights reflecting off a silver screen (the movie itself) can evoke emotional and psychological terror and/or delight from the audience. While we are viewing a movie, the unconscious forces of the psyche kick in. The overly simplified way to describe the strong impact of the example movie is this: since the viewer's psyche is left with an unresolved conflict that was imprinted upon it by the movie's final image of a fist in the air, it will then search for a resolution either internally or externally. A symbolic or actual victory or act of survival or courage must play out somewhere to balance the viewer's internal conflict.

The easiest way this conflict resolution may play out happens when an actual event reminds the viewer of a scene from the movie and that memory gives the person the impetus or courage to do something they normally would not have done. For example, they might describe their solution to this internal conflict by describing this or a similar situation: "The door stuck when I tried to push it open and I almost gave up. But then I thought of that scene from the movie and I body-slammed the door and it opened!" or "A stranger cried out for help and I wouldn't normally have gone to her aid, but I thought of that movie that I had seen and there I was running to help her." Many variations of this theme could play out as "psychic compensation" for the unresolved symbol of defeat implanted in the viewer's psyche by the movie. As I said in the Masculine/Feminine chapter (Fundamental Six), the psyche is always attempting to balance itself.

Sometimes those attempts at balance are played out externally, in ways that represent the person's internal struggle.

Now, let's relate this back to putting our interest or attention on a problem or issue. If you "get interested" in an unsolved personal conflict or problem, you engage your internal psychology, which will mysteriously go to work, helping out behind the scenes.

I believe this explains why clients in the process of working on themselves often experience what are called "synchronistic" events that duplicate a lesson or insight they have been working on in their therapy or coaching sessions. What does that mean? I am about to explain. Synchronistic events are actual, physical events that seem to "coincidentally" duplicate in the outside world the same issue we are dealing with in our internal psychological world. These events can duplicate and/or address problems, or even offer hints about them or solutions to them. These events can take many forms. Have you ever unexpectedly run into someone you needed an answer from but had not been able to reach for a while? Have you ever pulled a magazine off a rack while standing in a grocery store line and flipped it open, stunned that the article on that page is talking about the issues with which you are currently struggling? Or has someone told you about a problem they resolved and it seems that their solution would solve your issue? These are examples of synchronicity at work.

Let's spend another moment on this explanation and look at how synchronicity can show up when we are working on an issue in therapy or coaching. Let's say Sally (yes, the poor dear is back!) is working on the issue of how dismissive she is of others. For the next week, she finds herself mysteriously, glaringly and annoyingly surrounded by dismissive people. This forces her to experience the negative affects of being ignored, offering her the opportunity to get in touch with the impact of her behavior.

Ralph, on the other hand, has been working on some specific fears. He keeps noticing that people are talking to him about similar fears they too have experienced—even if they had never shared at such a deep, personal level before. Although coincidences such as these can often have a strange quality to them, they are actually external representations that come our way because they mirror or address the exact issues we are working on internally.

Here is another great example of this phenomenon that was recently related to me by a client of mine. James (not his real name), is a retired, super-achieving millionaire. He is now at a spiritual crossroads, because he has achieved everything he ever dreamed of since he was twenty years old—and he is only in his late 40's. Success has come to him much earlier than he had planned, and now he feels adrift in his life. "Is this all there is?" is a consuming question for him at this phase of his development. Although James may appear to "have it really good" from the outside, he has one major issue that is keeping him from enjoying his good fortune. This issue, which has become a block to his coaching progress, is his total avoidance of **feelings**. Intellectually, James understands this issue and the impact it is having on him, but he still cannot seem to find the courage to express his emotions openly. Feeling stuck, he decides to take a break from coaching to do some personal work on this issue.

After a few weeks, he phoned me rather excitedly to say that he had a weird story to tell me. (Now remember, when the psyche is stuck and feeling unresolved, it starts "mysteriously" trying to work the problem out in some way.) We meet and he tells me this story:

One day he had some free time and, armed with two newspapers, walked into a local cafe for a leisurely lunch. As he reached the entrance, he met a young man in his twenties, who is also on his way into the restaurant. They both paused and looked at each other. Then, James, with a dramatic flair, said "Let me open this grand door for you, my good young man," and pulled it open. The twenty-something laughed, walked through the door ahead of James and made his way to the bar. James tucked himself into a quiet booth, spread out his newspapers, ordered his lunch, and settled in for some extended reading time. A few minutes passed.

Then, the twenty-something walked over to James' booth and asked tenuously if he could join him. James, shocked but curious, agreed. To make a long story a bit shorter, the twenty-something proceeded to tell James his life story, including the fact that he has just broken up with his fiancé and that he is devastated. He says his life feels totally empty. He feels like a complete failure with women, and his career feels like it is over before it has even begun. As he is talking, he begins to cry. Keep in mind, they were complete strangers just twenty minutes earlier.

You can imagine the extreme discomfort the emotionally avoidant James must have been feeling during this total stranger's tearful exchange. To add to the synchronicity of this event, the twenty-something was the same age James was when he divorced his first wife. And, oddly enough, both men had ended their relationships because their wives had been sexually unfaithful. What a "coincidence." But there is more. James and the twenty-something both felt their careers were over too soon, and neither could imagine where their lives would go from here. The twenty-something was speaking about exactly the same issues that James was struggling with—and expressing the level of emotions James could not.

To finish the story, James very nervously gave a brief pep talk to the twenty-something in order to send him quickly on his way, paid the check for their drinks, and "got the hell outta there." He even made a point to pay the check with cash to make sure there were no identifying names or numbers that would allow this "kid" to contact him again.

From actual event

James laughed hysterically while he was telling me this story. Even he saw that something very out of the ordinary had played out that afternoon. How could this total stranger come over, pour his heart out, and cry about conflicts so similar to his?

Once again, the answer is psychic compensation. James was so stuck in his own psychological conflicts, and yet so interested in them, that his psyche began trying to help him out by attempting to compensate for his internal discomfort. How often have we been deeply troubled by a situation when suddenly just the right person has shown up to help us through the issue? Have you had an experience where just the right person called at just the right time to offer you just the right comforting or wise words? Or has someone near you unexpectedly blurted out a solution to your issue at just the right moment? Whether or not we understand it or acknowledge it, the psyche is constantly trying to balance out our issues, and to help us in unseen ways.

Let's get back to James for a minute. He was noticeably shaken after telling his story, even though it had happened days before. "What do I do with this weird event?" he asked, laughing nervously. "I mean that is some weird stuff…it's crazy!"

Since the event had definitely gotten James' attention, and his question showed that he was interested enough to spend some time figuring this out, I decided to approach my answer creatively. As a side note, I decided to go deeper in my analysis of this event than I would usually go with my coaching clients. Because most of the coaching clients I see are high masculine, super-achievers (including the women), they are usually not interested in deep symbolism. Interpreting this type of event at the level that I thought would be helpful to James would sound too "woo-woo" to most clients. But, when I focused on James, sitting in front of me, sincerely asking "why," in this particular circumstance I felt it was important to give him an answer commensurate to the level of the "weirdness" he was feeling about the event. I decided to take the risk, even though I feared he would probably label me as some far out, Californian, incense burning, tree hugger from that day forward.

To totally avoid that risk, I could have easily said, "This event is simply your psyche playing out your internal conflict for you in the external world through a process called psychic compensation," and watched him give me a fake nod of comprehension. But, as I said, I decided to answer his questions in a manner that would hopefully be more meaningful for him. In previous sessions, James had shown an interest in dream interpretation, so I asked him, "How would you interpret this event if it were simply a dream you were telling me about?"

He paused and then methodically re-told the story. We re-analyzed it as if it were a dream. It went something like this: He unexpectedly met a twenty-something at a doorway and offered to open the door for him. The stranger was about the same age as James had been when he was divorced. James "offered to open a door to enter a place where he was going to be for a while."

I added my interpretation: the "twenty-something" inside of James was coming forward now to express the emotion about his past and present that he could not previously express. James had, through his own psychological work, opened the door for his internal twenty-something, who had walked through that door into a new awareness.

Approaching this incident creatively in this way allowed James to do more with the event than just write it off as some "weird stuff." He realized that the twenty-something at the cafe mirrored his own internal twenty-something who had never grieved the loss of his first wife. The same twenty-something probably thought that becoming a millionaire would bring him total happiness later in life. He was taken by surprise when he achieved financial independence before the age of 50—leaving him with a feeling of emptiness and a lot of time on his hands.

I explained to James that synchronicity, brought forth through psychic compensation, had played out an event in front of him that mirrored his own internal conflicts. The similarities of the twenty something's issues and James' issues were too strong to chalk up to mere chance. There was a deeper reason these two men had been drawn together. The event showed him the missing element that would carry him to the next step of resolution——emotional expression. From that place of emotional work, something else, some new healing process and solution, can evolve.

This story is just one of the many examples that illustrate how our psyche, through psychic compensation, will go to work for us. If we are truly **interested** and engaged in our own growth process, whether we are moving forward at the moment or truly stuck, our psyche will often play out in dreams or in our external reality both the problem and workable solutions. Stop for a moment and just think of the power in this statement. If we just pay attention, solutions will reveal themselves to us! Amazing!

As a change agent, I have witnessed again and again the power of becoming interested in your own issues. Repeatedly, I have seen confirmation that when you put your attention and interest on something, both conscious and unconscious forces are put into play. But, alas, although mystical and magical forces sit waiting to assist everyone, only a minority will truly become interested in their issues. Unfortunately, most clients just do not want to be bothered by it all. "Isn't there some pill I can take?" they ask, only half jokingly. And I am left staring at my original problem—how to motivate clients to become interested in their issues.

So, if you are a reader who has become interested in your issues, "Well done," I say! You have taken the first step toward healing. You are on your way, and my advice to you is simple: focus on the part of you or the issues that you want to change. See the good outcome you want to reach, and then pay attention to where that leads you. Jot down insights and "Ah Ha" moments. Ask others if they have experienced similar awarenesses (and watch their funny expressions). If asking them about personal experiences seems inappropriate, simply ask them for "information".

If, for example, you want to find out how unaware you are of others, start by asking your spouse or partner how aware **they** think you are. They are usually great resources because they are chock-full of opinions about you! They may even have been keeping notes, for all you know! Then, after you have convinced yourself that they are absolutely wrong and unfairly biased against you, try playing another interesting game called, "What if they are absolutely right?" Are you interested enough to push through this ego-deflating portion of the interest game?

Most people are not. Yet some will look around at the landscape when it has been lit up after a light bulb goes on. Why do most people keep their eyes focused on the narrow path of denial, survival and status quo? Why is complaining more popular than curiosity? And why do people live passionless lives rather than attempt to live more fully?

Carl Jung, the famous psychologist and philosopher, said that laziness is the most prevalent psychological state. Most people would rather ignore the world than be interested in it. Interest requires time, energy, and focus. Sometimes giving these things to an issue can require discipline and, yes—good old hard work. Yet, interest, which is the foundation for passion, can be the spark that gets things rolling.

Final Thoughts

So there you have it! Nine Fundamentals of Human Behavior that describe why people do some crazy things. I am assuming that several things have probably happened while you were reading this book:

1. You have identified with some of the examples I have used because you have either done them yourself or seen them acted out by other people.

2. You have thought of several behaviors or incidents that are related to a Fundamental, but you are not sure whether they truly fit a particular Fundamental.

3. You have thought up some of your own Fundamentals that describe some behaviors in others you know.

You also may have come up with some questions about the Fundamentals. You may disagree with some of my wilder expansions on a few of them—such as the reason people slow down when they come to a wreck on the road and why there are so many skinny models in Hollywood. Whether you have questions and/or disagreements, I consider this to be, as they say, "all good."

Remember, I said in the beginning that my hope for this book is that it will lead to questions and discussions with several thoughtful friends over coffee or cocktails one slow afternoon. Questions such as:

"Which Fundamentals did you identify with?"

"Wasn't that last bit about traffic a little far fetched?"

"Doesn't that Fundamental fit Jenny to a tee?"

Agree or disagree with them, it is through thought and discussion that the many subtle variations and examples of the Fundamentals begin to appear.

Now that we are at the end of the book, I have a special bonus for you: one final Fundamental, which we will call the "bonus" Fundamental. I did not include this one with the others because it is not really broad enough to be included as a main Fundamental. However, now that you have finished the book, you might consider if it does apply to you or others. It is important enough to be included because this Fundamental can potentially undermine working with the other nine Fundamentals. What is this extremely powerful Fundamental, you ask? The BONUS Fundamental is:

Everyone wants to be the Exception.

If you have ever attended a presentation or a talk or a support group about a topic that involves human behavior, inevitably one of the first questions that is asked is:

"You are certainly not implying that if someone does (**this or that**), that they have to be (**this or that**), are you?"

or

"So, are you saying that if I do (**this**), then it makes me (**that**)? Because that is not true at all for me..."

Questions like these are inevitably asked to begin a distancing of oneself from the relevance of the material as it pertains to them personally. All variations of, "This cannot apply to me!" Here are some of my favorites that have come up while I have been discussing or presenting material from this book. These questions and statements often come across as exaggerations and they often get chuckles from the audience.

"Are you saying that because I slow down for a wreck on the side of the road that I am some kinda psychological wreck?"

or

"You're saying that because I watch sports on Sunday I hate women?"

or, (and I can't wait for this one because I **will** hear it)

A large hulk of a man asks:

"This whole Masculine/Feminine thing…are you saying I'm a homosexual?"

In my experience, the first people to ask questions are those who are trying to prove that they are exceptions to whatever rule, behavior, situation or, in this case, Fundamental you are discussing—especially if you are trying to make broad generalizations about people's psychological motivations or behavior. Everybody wants to be the exception. Before the basic description of a behavior is out of my mouth, people's egos are getting ruffled. Their minds are immediately rejecting the possibility that this applies to them. They start an internal dialogue that begins to list reasons that prove that it doesn't.

Why do audiences, workshop attendees, group members or friends inevitably do this? The primary reason is that it is terrifying to be seen/exposed by others. If we fall into some category that explains us, we feel seen by others, and that is more than a little bit unnerving. Actually, most people find it terrifying (see Fundamental One).

The two most intense fears identified by people on surveys are death and public speaking. Guess which one ranks as number one? If you guessed death, you are wrong. Why, then, would public speaking be more frightening than death? Because when someone is speaking to an audience, they are being looked at, and examined, by others. They are exposed. They are being seen. From this information, we can see that being exposed or seen is the most terrifying experience that most people can imagine.

People deal with this fear by establishing (usually by using numerous examples and justifications), for everyone's benefit, that: "I am NOT that—that is not ME—that may be you, but it is not ME! I am mysterious." If we are mysterious then no one can figure us out; therefore we cannot be seen. If we cannot be seen, we are safe.

I have a personal example that shows this fear in action. Whenever I am out socially with people I am meeting for the first time, inevitably the question of work comes up, and people ask me what I do for a living. I hate this question. When I tell them I am a psychotherapist, nine times out of ten, people jump back and/or gasp (literally). "Oh, my GOD," they say, "You're not gonna psychoanalyze ME, are you?" Fear races across their faces. I assure them that I will not, and they usually avoid me for the rest of the event. The majority of people find the thought of possibly being analyzed (seen by someone else) terrifying and they avoid the possibility of that happening by distancing themselves from me.

When I make broad generalizations for the sake of discussion and impact, as I have throughout this book, the more terrified someone is by the information, the more they will feel the need to make themselves the exception. (Remember, if I am the exception, then you do not see me, and you cannot explain me; therefore I am safe.) Since everyone is terrified (Fundamental One), everyone wants to be safe. Therefore everyone wants to be the exception to any thought, idea, or concept that attempts to expose their inner thoughts, feelings or motivations.

Please realize that when I use the words "everyone" or "usually" in this book, I am doing so purposefully as a tool to push you past your comfort level. Maybe, just maybe, Fear truly is a universal psychological underpinning that we all experience to varying degrees at various times of the day—**every**day. See I did it again. I use the extreme language simply to stretch the envelope of awareness that is **usually** available to you.

Now back to our Bonus Fundamental. While there are **many** genuine exceptions to each of these Fundamentals, seeing yourself as an exception greatly lessens your opportunity to benefit from the insights that any of the Fundamentals can give you. To make the best use of what you have just spent hours reading and thinking through, are you willing to try an experiment? There is an alternative way of approaching your most likely "knee jerk" reaction to the Fundamentals. Instead of immediately declaring, "No, that definitely does not apply to me!" why not try: "Maybe it does, in some instances." (Trust me, you can always go back to "No!" anytime you wish.) For the sake of expanding your viewpoint and perspective just a little, why not give "Maybe" a try as you discuss the Fundamentals with your friends over coffee or cocktails. Once you automatically respond with "NO," you have stopped the possibility of discussion. If you say "Maybe," discussion can continue.

Since I have waited until the very last chapter of this book to suggest that you consider giving the "maybe" approach a try, you have probably already identified those Fundamentals that do not apply to you. This is a natural reaction and should be expected.

So in the very near future, when I begin giving talks to bigger and bigger audiences, and I inevitably hear this question:

"You say in your first Fundamental that everyone is terrified, but I am NOT EVER terrified... how do you explain that?"

Since I know people do some crazy things, I will simply say,

"You are obviously the exception to the rule."

Call me crazy.

Food For Thought

Fundamental One

Everyone is terrified and therefore unreliable…until they're not.

Remember the last time you got angry at someone or at some event. Can you identify the underlying fear you had about what happened or could have happened because of what they did?

Remember the last time a friend or associate got angry at you. What was the underlying fear they may have had behind the anger? What could they have lost: reputation, status, respect? What might have been embarrassing for them, real or imagined, because of the incident?

Have you ever been violent physically with someone? What was your fear in that moment? Did you stand to lose something? Was your standing or status with them diminished in some way?

When did you last scream at someone? Did you feel your opinion was not being heard or was being discounted? Is this a fear you have had before in the relationship? Can you talk to them directly about this fear and the need to be heard by them?

We often scream out of fear at children who are about to hurt themselves. They often cry or strike back out of fear in *reaction* to our anger. Can you identify a time you screamed at a friend because you thought they were about to hurt themselves? Was their potential damage physical? Was it psychological, like in repeating a relational mistake? What was your fear for them and what gave it such urgency (the anger) for you?

Fundamental Two

No one wants you to succeed too well or fail too badly

Name some friends over the years that have reacted differently to you because of a success or failure. (Examples: A job promotion, a new house, car, boy/girlfriend, child anything new or any new success. OR… a job loss, a bankruptcy, a divorce, a death or the loss of anything.) How did they act differently around you? Did they simply avoid you? Did their behavior change over time or get back to normal?

Name some friends **you** have felt jealous over because of a big success they had. Did the jealousy eventually subside? Did it subside because of a success you yourself eventually had? Are there any friends you have felt uncomfortable around because of a loss they experienced? Were you unsure how to help or afraid of their pain, grief?

Have you ever lost a friend because of a new boy/girlfriend? Were the friends single at the time? Have you ever lost a friend because you married? Have you ever been jealous of someone else's dating or marriage partner? Did you ever hope the relationship wouldn't last?

When was the last time a friend complimented you on something new you got? Did you notice that as the price of the new item goes up the compliments go down? For example: new clothes get complimented regularly but not new cars, houses, boats. Did you notice that after the first initial viewing, compliments later on are extremely rare or non-existent? How often do **you** compliment others on their purchases or accomplishments? Did you repeat the compliment at a later date?

Fundamental Three

Genuine Interest in and Attention to Others is a Rare Commodity

When was the last time a friend of yours did **not** acknowledge or thank you for a gift, kindness, favor, or contribution you gave them? Is it a close friend? Is this lack of acknowledgement typical?

When was the last time a friend of yours acknowledged or thanked you for something kind you did for them? Is this a friend that usually thanks you for the things you do? How often do **you** give praise for someone else's accomplishment or new purchase? Do you do it more than once?

When was the last time a total stranger thanked you for a kindness (example: opening a door for them, picking something up for them)? When was the last time **you** thanked a total stranger for something? Have you ever made a stranger smile or laugh? Do you ever smile at strangers?

When was the last time someone waved nicely at you for letting their car enter your line of traffic? Do you wave when someone lets you in? When was the last time someone pulled in front of your car **without** giving any kind acknowledgement?

Have you ever felt ignored by others at a gathering? Do you talk to the majority of people you see at a party? If not, why? Could they feel ignored by you?

Do you speak kindly to wait staff at restaurants? Do you ever ask how their day is, or do you just order your food? What type of people are unworthy of your interest or attention: cashiers, janitors, strangers, people of other races? Why?

Fundamental Four

Most relationships, and their recurring problems, are based on power dynamics.

In which relationships, personal, or professional do you compete with others? Is it innocent for fun or serious for status, reputation or power? Does losing interfere with friendly interactions afterward? Have you ever felt someone was too serious about winning? How did it affect your interactions?

Have you ever used sex (by either refusing it or offering it) to get your way or feel powerful? Have you ever sexually frustrated someone just to feel powerful or for revenge? Have you ever felt manipulated sexually by someone else?

Have you ever angrily used the expression, "YOUR son'" or "YOUR daughter" to your spouse? What made you want to be superior to your spouse in that situation? What seemingly inferior behavior were you distancing yourself from?

Do you have trouble asking directly for what you want rather than feeling that you need to prove someone OWES it to you? Have you ever coerced someone to do something for you by making them feel bad? Has someone ever done that to you? How did it affect your relationship with them? Did you want to avoid them?

Do you know anyone who uses their anger to control situations? Do they have a reputation for it or was it a one time experience? Have you ever used anger to push people away?

Who have you perceived as powerful people in your life? What made them powerful? Was their power based on their ability to manipulate others or from their own positive achievements? Were they loved by others or feared?

Fundamental Five

Everyone is rushing for the white picket fence.

Can you think of any friends that you feel married too early or young? What made you think that? Did they have areas in their lives that would improve if they got married? How old were you when you knew you wanted to get married? How many years did you wait?

Have you ever felt you were being interviewed on a date about your marriage potential? Have you ever interviewed someone about their marriage potential on a date? How did they react? Have you ever felt that being in a relationship with someone without marriage potential is a waste of your time? If yes, have you ever thought that experiencing relationships of different types is the only way to learn and mature in relationships?

How did you decide on your career? Did other people influence your decision? How? What would be your dream career? Have you ever considered a career change? How old were you?

How old were you when you decided you wanted to have children? How long did you wait? Did you ever imagine an entire life without children? Do you know anybody over twenty who does? What do you think of people who do not want children?

What does your ideal of the "white picket fence" look like? Have you changed that ideal over time? What would it look like now? Do you feel stuck in an old fantasy and how would you change it if you could?

Have you ever known someone who threw away their respected "white picket fence" life for a "strange" life? Did they regret it or were they happier?

Fundamental Six

The Immature Masculine tries to run from or dominate the Feminine.

Which masculine personality characteristics do you portray in your life? Which feminine personality characteristics do you portray? (Let your friends help you with this) Do you see yourself as masculine dominant or feminine dominant? How do your friends see you? Are the dominant traits opposite of your gender? Does this awareness make you uncomfortable? How and why?

Which of your friends seem to have masculine dominant personality characteristics while being female gendered and which have feminine dominant personality characteristics while being masculine gendered? Which friends match in both personality and gender? Can you think of any friends who have changed in personality (M/F) dominance over time? What do you think contributed to this? Have you changed over time?

Think of your friends in relationships. Who has the most masculine personality and who has the most feminine personality in each relationship? Do their genders match their characteristics? Can you think of any relationships lasting over six months where both people have masculine dominant personalities or feminine dominant personalities?

Do you have friends who are uncomfortable with the idea that they could have an opposite gender than their personality reflects? What makes them uncomfortable with it?

Fundamental Seven

Everyone points the finger.

What event, person, subject makes you the most angry? Can you boil this down to its fundamental underlying theme? This can be tricky for everyone so here are a few examples of the types of the negative themes that come forward: sexual promiscuity, taking advantage of another, hurting someone weaker, dominating another with power, manipulation of others, being unfair or thoughtless. They do not always have to be negative themes either, for example themes can include: tenderness, loving, vulnerability, softness. Ever watch a man angrily berate a boy for being "soft" or a "fairy"—that is anger (fear) at the theme of tenderness. Once you find the theme (this is tricky also), can you find the similarity of that theme to a similar behavior you do? It is usually best to start this exercise thinking of a friend and a subject that makes their blood boil. Can you identify the theme underlying that subject? Now how and where have you seen or heard them doing a similar behavior. Sometimes it is in private, but usually the behavior is acted out in some area of their lives. Remember, their way of acting out the behavior they get so angry about is always slightly different than the behavior they are pointing at.

For example, someone may get furious when they see a pet slapped, but slap their kids regularly or someone who hates their boss for micro managing them, but is totally domineering when they get home.

Think of some recent public scandals in the news (politicians are great for examples of the pointing finger). Ever notice the upsurge of gay bashing politicians and religious leaders who themselves are caught in gay sexual situations? How about policeman doing criminal behavior while complaining about all the crooks out there? Ever notice the biggest flirts are the first to point at "whores" and "sluts"? What about "Right to Life" proponents who kill abortion doctors? Any other examples come to mind?

Fundamental Eight

We all have multiple personalities.

Have you ever seen your partner or friends interact with their parents? Did they act differently or show a different personality than you had seen before? Were they the "rebellious child" personality or maybe the "pampered angel" personality? Has your partner ever seen you act differently around your parents?

Have you ever called a friend, spouse at work or met them at work? Did they have a different demeanor or personality? Has anyone commented on how you are different at work than at home?

Think of your past relationships. Did certain partners bring out different personalities? Which one do you not see as often these days? Are there personalities that only you have seen alone?

Have alcohol or drugs brought out personalities that only show themselves when you are using them? What are those personalities like? Are they ones you would like to access more often or hope to never see again?

What is your personality like around your children? Is it different than with your friends or at your workplace? Have you ever seen different personalities in your children? What situations brought them out?

How many personalities can you identify in yourself? How many of these have your partner or friends seen? What is the most recent one you have encountered? What extra skills, mind-sets, or mannerisms do some of them have that are especially useful?

Fundamental Nine

We are all addicted to intensity.

What activities give you the biggest rush? Is it a substance? Does it involve physical exertion? Is it a psychological thrill? How often do you engage in them?

Think of a friend you have that is always in crisis. Do they seem to exaggerate every problem? Do they seem to enjoy the attention they get from the crisis? Have you ever gotten an adrenaline pumping rush from a crisis? Did it feel invigorating for a while?

Do you know of anyone who regularly takes physical risks as part of their hobbies? Do they take psychological risks in their relationships? How do your friends get their rush? How often do you drink coffee, caffeine or energy drinks? How do you react without them?

How often do you feel bored? What do you do to relieve it? How often are you able to sit in a chair and simply read or do a crossword puzzle or knit? How many activities are you usually doing when you sit down to watch television? Can you sit still long enough to watch an entire movie?

Who is the black sheep in your family? Does there seem to be an odd favoritism by your parents toward him/her? Do they complain about him/her while bending over backwards to help? Are they the constant topic of discussion?

Do you have any friends who are in negative relationships? Do they complain and complain, but not do anything to change them? Are the stories starting to get repetitive and boring?

Invite The Author To Your Own Discussion Party!

As the purpose of this book is to encourage discussions, Kevin Davis will attend any discussion party, or Question and Answer session you plan with your own neighborhood book club or discussion groups. Available in person in the Metro Atlanta area, he is also available by conference call (speakerphone/webcam) to any group nationwide looking to further discuss the book or ask questions about the Fundamentals of Human Behavior. These discussion sessions are usually an hour in length and are free of charge for a limited time to all groups of five or more. Contact the author at his website: **phonecoachlive.com** for further information. He can also be reached at Corporate Coaching International (404) 262-3368.

Index